FLORENCE TRAVEL GUIDE

Captivating Adventures through Renaissance Masterpieces,

Tuscan Beauty, Florentine Landmarks, Hidden Gems, and More

© **Copyright 2024 - All rights reserved.**

The content contained within this book may not be reproduced, duplicated, or transmitted without direct written permission from the author or the publisher.

Under no circumstances will any blame or legal responsibility be held against the publisher, or author, for any damages, reparation, or monetary loss due to the information contained within this book, either directly or indirectly.

Legal Notice:

This book is copyright protected. It is only for personal use. You cannot amend, distribute, sell, use, quote, or paraphrase any part, or the content within this book, without the consent of the author or publisher.

Disclaimer Notice:

Please note the information contained within this document is for educational and entertainment purposes only. All effort has been executed to present accurate, up-to-date, reliable, and complete information. No warranties of any kind are declared or implied. Readers acknowledge that the author is not engaging in the rendering of legal, financial, medical, or professional advice. The content within this book has been derived from various sources. Please consult a licensed professional before attempting any techniques outlined in this book.

By reading this document, the reader agrees that under no circumstances is the author responsible for any losses, direct or indirect, that are incurred as a result of the use of the information contained within this document, including, but not limited to, errors, omissions, or inaccuracies.

Welcome Aboard, Discover
Your Limited-Time Free Bonus!

Hello, traveler! Welcome to the Captivating Travels family, and thanks for grabbing a copy of this book! Since you've chosen to join us on this journey, we'd like to offer you something special.

Check out the link below for a FREE Ultimate Travel Checklist eBook & Printable PDF to make your travel planning stress-free and enjoyable.

But that's not all - you'll also gain access to our exclusive email list with even more free e-books and insider travel tips. Well, what are you waiting for? Click the link below to join and embark on your next adventure with ease.

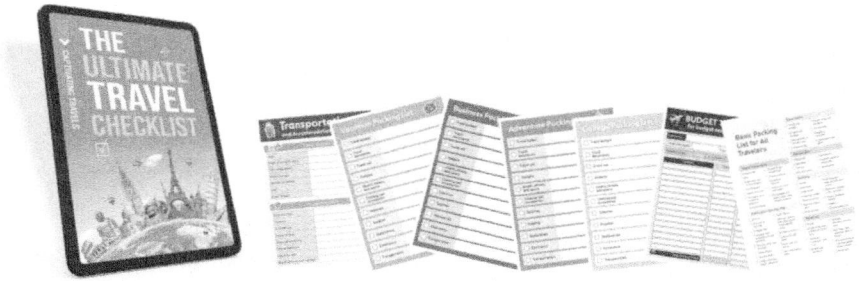

Access your bonus here: https://livetolearn.lpages.co/checklist/

Or, Scan the QR code!

TABLE OF CONTENTS

Introduction 5

Chapter 1: Get to Know Florence 7

Chapter 2: To and From the Airport 21

Chapter 3: Rifredi 26

Chapter 4: Isolotto-Legnaia 41

Chapter 5: Campo di Marte 51

Chapter 6: Centro Storico 64

Chapter 7: Gavinana-Galluzzo 89

Chapter 8: City Itineraries and Programs 102

Chapter 9: Day Trips Beyond the City 142

Bonus Chapter: Useful Survival Phrases 157

Appendix 165

Here's another book by Captivating Travels
that you might like 176

Welcome Aboard, Discover Your Limited-Time Free Bonus! . . . 177

References 178

Image Resources 184

INTRODUCTION

Florence is a city of architectural beauty, artistic brilliance, political revelations, and a cultural treasure trove. It is the heart of Italy, which pumps life-giving blood to the rest of the landscape, enhancing it beyond imagination. This book will lay the city bare before you, from helping you explore its most popular destinations to leading you through its unheard-of streets.

Florence map.[1]

You will begin with an overview of Florence, its history, evolution to modernity, people, culture, cuisine, transportation options, and so much more. How can you reach the city? How do you get from the airport to the city center?

What are the average rates for traveling within Florence? In short, you will be introduced to its outer, most visible layer. Only then will each individual layer be peeled until you finally get a look at its beating heart. The guide is divided into individual districts for easy reading.

The first layer will reveal Rifredi – the north-northwest part of Florence, in its raw form. It has several popular and less-known sights to explore. You will proceed to behold Isolotto e Legnaia, which lies to the west-southwest. This is where you will meet the transcendent Arno River and a number of other bonnie little things.

To the east lies Campo di Marte – an entirely different part of Florence brimming with various activities. Feel free to observe stars in the tranquil night with a guided tour, or you may even catch your favorite music band in action at its vast stadium.

Then, you will proceed to Centro Storico – the heart of the heart (Florence) to marvel at everything that gives the city its reputation. It is a treat for the artistically inclined. The final layer to be peeled is Gavinana-Galluzzo, which is to the south, with peaceful neighborhoods and a captivating atmosphere.

An exhaustive itinerary for each region follows that will take you through Florence along the most scenic routes and at the best times. The penultimate chapter details a few exotics, must-see locations a little beyond the borders of the city. The book ends with a long list of useful survival phrases for those who don't know the local language. They are sure to help you out of a pickle.

It is a comprehensive book in easy-to-understand language that will arm you with all the information regarding Florence and more. First-time travelers will find it thoroughly enlightening, and repeat tourists are bound to find a few good things they missed the first time around.

CHAPTER 1
GET TO KNOW FLORENCE

Florence is a city of wonders. It is a hub of fantastic art and architecture, and it houses a rich and varied cultural and political history of Italy. This is where the Renaissance began, transforming it into a place where high-end fashion flourishes today. The city pulled the world out of the turbulent Middle Ages to herald the dawn of the modern era. If you wish to get to know Florence, look at its revolutionary history, experience its peculiar culture, and take in its breathtaking sights and architecture. Indeed, Florence is a city that stands apart from any other city. It is a world unto itself.

GEOGRAPHICAL LOCATION

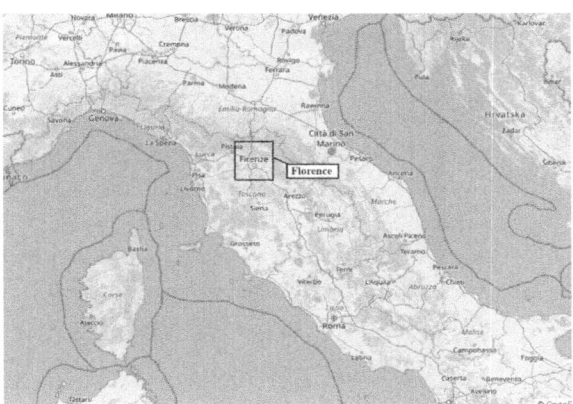

Florence (Firenze).[2]

Florence is a center of not just arts and culture but also politics, commerce, economics, finance, and fashion. It is pronounced as "Firenze" by the locals, like the iconic centaur from the Harry Potter books. It is the capital of Tuscany; a region in Italy known for its exemplary beauty. A multitude of glorious hillside towns and structures surround the city, from Fiesole and Settignano in the east, to Arcetri in the south.

The Arno River flows through the city, along with a few smaller streams like Mugnone and Greve. Florence was first founded and developed into a city to control a prime crossing across the Arno River during the Roman era. Nevertheless, being an important milestone for getting from Rome to Bologna, it used to be prone to attack. Huge walls were built to protect the inhabitants from such eventualities in the 12th century, but they were demolished during the 19th century to make way for urbanization. However, the remains of those once-formidable walls can still be found in many parts of Florence today.

CLIMATE

The perfect time to Florence is during spring and fall. Its summers can be extremely hot and humid, and its winters sometimes experience snowfall, which covers the city's architectural beauty. Extreme temperatures may range from 30° (-1°C) in the winter to 95° (35°C). The cold showers post-winter are another factor to consider, which may begin to become extreme in April. The ideal time to visit Florence is in March, when the weather is pleasantly sunny and warm, and in early September, when there is a light chill in the air.

BACKGROUND HISTORY

Florence was initially called "Florentia" or "the flourishing town" back when it was founded in the Roman era (circa 59 BCE). Nobody probably believed it would flourish, however, because it was primarily occupied by the soldiers of the Roman army. Against all odds, it became the home of "Mars," a Roman deity, along with numerous public baths. Around that time, when a major amphitheater was constructed, the small town began to flourish, developing into a provincial capital of the Roman Empire in the 3rd century CE.

Despite Florence's rising commercial significance, it changed hands quite a few times in the later years, from the Ostrogoths in the 5th century to the Byzantines a hundred years later. It wasn't until the Countess Matilda began her rule of Tuscany that it transformed into a thriving city in the late 11th century.

Thereafter, Florence slowly developed into a formidable economic and political force in the region, with its textile and banking sectors as backbones. By the start of the 14th century, it had become the apple of Italy's eye and grew into one of the greatest cities in the whole of Europe. However, its hard-earned power and fame weren't meant to last long.

The year was 1348, when the Black Death, the worst pandemic of all time, struck Florence and wiped out half of its population. The rest of Europe wasn't spared either, but Florence tumbled down an abyss of despair it would not recover from for more than 50 years. During the city's prime, it was ruled by seven powerful guilds, but after the destruction wrought by the Black Death pandemic, nobody knew who was in charge. Amid this chaos, a new power gradually emerged. Bankers and merchants caught the reins of politics and culture, specifically Cosimo de' Medici, whose family would go on to transform the face of Florence and, in turn, the entirety of Europe.

The Medici family didn't need any official title to rule Florence. [3]

The Medici family didn't need any official title to rule Florence. They governed the masses by virtue of their seemingly unending wealth owing to their powerful banking institutions. It marked nearly 50 years of peace in the city. The family was known for its patronage of arts and culture, which greatly flourished during their reign. Many tried to usurp their standing in the city over the years, but the Medicis always came back with a storm.

The family's line eventually dwindled down to Cosimo III (until 1723), whose son's death ended their rule once and for all. After being governed by outside rulers for more than a hundred years, Florence eventually became a part of the Kingdom of Italy, where it was assigned as its capital for six years. It was during these six years that its modern era began.

EVOLUTION TO THE MODERN TIMES

Being Italy's capital led to rapid growth in Florence's population (more than before the Black Death pandemic), as many people from other parts of the kingdom arrived in droves. The city may have held the position only for six years, but it remained an important region of Italy for several decades. During this time, the defensive walls surrounding it were torn down to facilitate easy commuting to and from Florence. Quite a few of its ancient architectural buildings were demolished to make way for modern structures. World War II saw the German troops destroying all its bridges, except for the now-famous Ponte Vecchio.

However, humans weren't the only ones responsible for Florence's intermittent destruction. The incessant floods from the Arno River have brought down many important landmarks and bridges over the centuries. The flood of 1966 was the most devastating of the lot when the water level rose to nearly 36 feet above ground in many places. Many ancient artworks and books were damaged beyond repair, but the rest of the world helped recover what they could.

Today, Florence has embraced the modern era while managing to preserve its rich history and culture. With the huge influx of tourists, pollution reached record highs in the 1980s, but the restricted driving rules that were implemented later brought down the levels a notch. Nevertheless, the city continues to cater to tourists, with between 10 to 16 million people visiting each year from all over the globe. Tuscany may have taken a giant leap into the technological age, but Florence remains the "museum city" even today.

CULTURAL RELATIONSHIP WITH OTHER ITALIAN REGIONS

Being the birthplace of the Renaissance, Florence's impact on arts, music, religion, politics, and literature has been immense, especially throughout Tuscany and the surrounding regions.

ART AND RENAISSANCE INFLUENCE

During the Renaissance, Florence became a hub for artistic innovation and cultural advancement. Artists like Leonardo da Vinci, Michelangelo, and Botticelli thrived in Florence, leaving behind a legacy that influenced all of Italy. Their works spread to various regions, impacting the artistic landscape nationwide. The movement's further impact on the whole of Europe is well known.

TRADE AND COMMERCE

Florence's economic prosperity in the Renaissance era was largely due to its flourishing trade and banking sectors. This economic influence extended beyond Tuscany, establishing connections with other regions like Venice, Rome, and Milan. The Medici family had a vast network of alliances and patronages across Italy, impacting the city's cultural and political dynamics.

ARCHITECTURE AND URBAN PLANNING

Florence's architectural marvels like the Cathedral of Santa Maria del Fiore (the Duomo), the Uffizi Gallery, and the Palazzo Vecchio, showcase innovative designs that influenced architecture throughout Italy. Architects and planners from Florence were in great demand in other regions, leaving their mark on various cities in the vicinity.

CUISINE

The Tuscan and Florentine cuisine's impact on the rest of Italy does not go unnoticed. It is known for its emphasis on simplicity, yet with high-quality ingredients. Dishes like ribollita (vegetable soup), bistecca alla Fiorentina (Florentine steak), and different kinds of pasta from the region have found their way into menus across Italy.

LITERATURE AND LANGUAGE

Florence, with its rich literary history and the use of the Tuscan dialect, played a crucial role in shaping the Italian language. Writers like Dante Alighieri, who wrote the epic poem "The Divine Comedy," used the Tuscan dialect, eventually becoming the basis for modern Italian. This linguistic influence spread across Italy, contributing to a unified national language.

Indeed, Florence has always been a center for cultural exchange. Scholars, artists, and intellectuals from around the nation and beyond congregated in Florence, fostering a vibrant cultural environment that facilitated the exchange of ideas and further influenced other parts of the country. Also, did you know that the Historic Center of Florence is a UNESCO World Heritage site?

INTERESTING FACTS ABOUT THE FLORENTINES

The people in Florence are friendly and good-natured, especially toward tourists. Among themselves, they often display a wry sense of humor that may seem rude and pessimistic to outsiders. They prize their self-worth and the artistic beauty of their city above all else. They are slightly different from other Italians in the sense that they prefer to keep to themselves. However, they love to socialize during their important traditions and festivals, which they are very proud of.

SCOPPIO DEL CARRO (EXPLOSION OF THE CART)

This amazingly fun tradition dates back to the Crusades and is held on Easter Sunday. A cart filled with fireworks is paraded through the streets of Florence and is ignited by a mechanical dove symbolizing the Holy Spirit. It is believed that a successful ignition brings good luck throughout the year.

GELATO

While not unique to Florence, gelato holds a special place in the city's culinary culture. This delicious dessert is believed to have originated in the city itself. Today, Florence has numerous gelaterias serving artisanal gelato made with fresh, high-quality ingredients. Indulging in this frozen treat is a beloved tradition for locals and tourists alike.

FEAST DAYS AND RELIGIOUS CELEBRATIONS

Various religious festivals and feast days are observed in Florence, with processions, parades, and special church services. Many events are marked by festivities, fireworks, and historical reenactments, like the Feast of San Giovanni (St. John the Baptist), the patron saint of Florence, which is celebrated on June 24 every year.

ARTISAN CRAFTS

Florence has a long tradition of artisanal craftsmanship, particularly in leatherworking, jewelry making, and artisanal paper production. There are a number of workshops and boutiques spread across the city, creating high-quality, handcrafted goods day in and day out.

APERITIVO

The Italian tradition of Aperitivo, which originated in northern Italy, is also embraced in Florence. In the early evening, locals gather in bars for pre-dinner drinks accompanied by small snacks or appetizers. Yes, the Florentines like to keep to themselves, but not during Aperitivo evenings!

HISTORICAL REENACTMENTS

Various historical reenactments, particularly linked to the Renaissance era, take place throughout the year, showcasing traditional clothing, music, and dances. These events often occur during special occasions or festivals and offer a glimpse into Florence's vibrant past.

PITTI IMMAGINE

This is not a historical tradition but a modern-day one. Pitti Immagine is a bi-annual fashion event that brings together designers, buyers, and fashion enthusiasts from around the world. Did you know that Gucci, a leading luxury fashion brand, was founded in the city? This yearly tradition shows how far Florence has come in revolutionizing art.

CUISINE

Of the top three things Florence is known for, one is bound to be its cuisine! With the numerous fresh ingredients that Tuscany is known for and the artistic acumen of the Florentines, you can expect every dish to taste uniquely different. Its flavors are slightly different from the rest of Italy because its food is primarily influenced by the Renaissance period. Here are a few must-try dishes at any restaurant in the city.

BISTECCA ALLA FIORENTINA

This is a famous Florentine dish containing a T-bone steak grilled and seasoned with salt, pepper, and sometimes olive oil. The steak is typically from the Chianina breed of cattle.

RIBOLLITA

Ribollita is the taste of Tuscany and, in turn, Florence. It's a delicious soup made with bread, cannellini beans, and vegetables (kale, cabbage, carrots, and onions), and it is often flavored with olive oil and herbs. It's usually cooked twice to create a thick and flavorful soup.

PAPPA AL POMODORO

This is a thick Florentine bread and tomato soup made with stale bread, tomatoes, garlic, basil, olive oil, and sometimes onions. It's a comforting dish in the colder months, and it can even be consumed chilled in the summer.

CROSTINI DI FEGATINI

This popular Florentine appetizer is a crostini (type of bread) topped with a spread made from chicken liver, butter, onion, and either capers or anchovies.

CANTUCCI AND VIN SANTO

Cantucci is an almond biscuit often served with Vin Santo, a sweet dessert wine. The traditional way to enjoy this dessert is by dipping the cantucci into the Vin Santo.

LAMPREDOTTO

This is a traditional Florentine dish made from the abomasum (fourth stomach of a cow), cooked in a broth, and served in a sandwich with green sauce or salsa verde.

CACIUCCO

It's a seafood stew hailing from Livorno, a port city near Florence, and it is made with various types of fish, shellfish, tomatoes, garlic, and red pepper flakes.

RICOTTA AND SPINACH RAVIOLI

Craving for classic Italian pasta? Try ricotta and spinach ravioli, a stuffed pasta filled with a mixture of fresh ricotta cheese and spinach, often served with a simple tomato sauce or sage and butter.

CHIANTI WINE

Florence is located in the Chianti region, famous for its red wine made primarily from Sangiovese grapes. Chianti is a popular local wine that can be sipped to wash down almost any Florentine dish.

SPORTS

The Florentines are massive sports buffs, so much so that they have their very own unique sport.

CALCIO STORICO FIORENTINO

This is a historic sport native to Florence, dating back to the 16th century. An eclectic mix of football, rugby, and wrestling, it is considered to be one of the most ruthless sports activities. It is played in traditional 16th-century costumes. Four teams representing different historical neighborhoods compete in this fierce and unique sport during special events held in Piazza Santa Croce.

FOOTBALL (SOCCER)

Like the rest of Italy, football is immensely popular in Florence. ACF Fiorentina is the city's main football club, and matches at the Stadio Artemio Franchi attract thousands of passionate local supporters during each game.

BASKETBALL

Florence also has a basketball presence. The city's teams, Fiorentina and Pallacanestro Firenze, compete in the Italian basketball league.

CYCLING

Tuscany, including Florence, offers beautiful landscapes and challenging terrain, making it a popular destination for cyclists. The region hosts cycling events and has numerous biking routes catering to both amateurs and professionals.

RUNNING AND MARATHONS

Florence hosts various running events and marathons throughout the year, attracting local and international participants. The Florence Marathon is a major annual event that draws professional runners from around the world.

RUGBY

While rugby might not be as popular as football in Italy, Florence has rugby clubs and enthusiasts who engage in the sport. Local clubs provide opportunities for both amateurs and serious players.

GYMNASTICS AND MARTIAL ARTS

Traditional Italian sports like gymnastics and martial arts have a healthy presence in Florence. There are clubs and schools offering training in disciplines such as judo, karate, and many types of gymnastics.

WATER SPORTS

Florence's inland location might make this seem like a surprising addition. However, the rivers and lakes present in the region offer ample opportunities for water sports like rowing, kayaking, and canoeing.

FAMOUS FLORENTINE FIGURES

Much of Florence's fame lies in the past, but it doesn't mean there aren't any well-known Florentines today. Some of the most famous names include:

DANTE ALIGHIERI

When it comes to arts and culture, Florence is the city to beat. The renowned poet and author of "The Divine Comedy," Dante Alighieri's name has to be first on the list. It is not without good reason that he is considered to be one of the greatest literary minds in history. Dante is often referred to as the father of the Italian language and literature.

LEONARDO DA VINCI

This quintessential Renaissance polymath is known for his contributions to art, science, engineering, and anatomy. Da Vinci's "Mona Lisa" and "The Last Supper" are major artworks that have been involved in fierce debates to this day. His scientific ideas were far beyond his time, but interestingly, he never published his theories.

MICHELANGELO BUONARROTI

As da Vinci is to the "Mona Lisa," Michelangelo is to "David," a colossal statue located in Via Ricasoli, Florence. This widely influential sculptor, painter, architect, and poet is also celebrated for other masterpieces like the frescoes in the Sistine Chapel and the design of St. Peter's Basilicas' dome in Rome.

GALILEO GALILEI

Florentine scientists are almost as acclaimed as their artists. The first name that springs to mind is Galileo Galilei, a pioneering astronomer, physicist, and mathematician. Who doesn't remember his epic free fall experiment from the Leaning Tower of Pisa? His space observations through a cutting-edge (for that age) telescope of his own creation revolutionized the human understanding of the cosmos.

NICCOLÒ MACHIAVELLI

A political philosopher, writer, and diplomat, Machiavelli is known for his work, "The Prince," a treatise on politics and power, which would go on to influence political thought for centuries. The term "Machiavellian (schemes, ideas, deeds, etc.)" comes from this Florentine. He was the first person to propose the concept that "the ends always justify the means."

GIOVANNI BOCCACCIO

An Italian author and poet, Boccaccio's notable work, "The Decameron," is a collection of one hundred novellas showcasing diverse narratives and themes.

AMERIGO VESPUCCI

An explorer and navigator, Vespucci is known for his voyages to the New World. Christopher Columbus may have discovered America, but the continent was named after Amerigo Vespucci because he was among the first ones to realize that they had landed not on the far shores of Asia – but on an entirely new landmass.

GIOTTO DI BONDONE

Giotto was an influential painter and architect. He is regarded as a pioneer of the Italian Renaissance and is known for his frescoes and contributions to art. Cimabue, the last of the Byzantine-style artists of Italy, along with another Florentine, is believed to have taught Giotto everything he knew.

CATHERINE DE MEDICI

The powerful Medici family of Florence was famous not only throughout Italy but also in France. Catherine de' Medici became Queen of France in 1547. Her reign was said to have been ruthless and bloody, with the massacre of French Huguenots on Bartholomew's Day and the plotting of a few subsequent wars.

ROBERTO CAVALLI

Among the famous Florentines still alive, Roberto Cavalli's name is known far and wide. He is a renowned Italian fashion designer known for his bold and glamorous designs, particularly in the realm of high-end clothing and accessories. Born on November 15, 1940, in Florence, Cavalli has had a significant impact on the fashion industry. His sand-blasted jeans style is popular in many parts of the world. His namesake brand caters to luxury clientele, selling not only clothing and accessories but also perfumes and jewelry.

GUCCIO GUCCI

Guccio Gucci was an Italian fashion designer and the founder of the renowned luxury fashion brand – *Gucci*. Born in 1881 in Florence, he established the House of Gucci at the age of 42. Initially, Gucci focused on producing high-quality leather goods, particularly luggage and accessories, gaining a reputation for craftsmanship and excellence. As the brand started gaining recognition, it expanded its offerings to include clothing, handbags, shoes, and other luxury items. Guccio Gucci's designs were inspired by his experiences and travels as he incorporated elements from equestrian sports. Some notable examples include the iconic horse bit and stirrup motifs that became synonymous with the Gucci brand.

RACHELE BRUNI

When you win any World Series thrice, your name is etched in history. That's exactly what Rachele Bruni, an athletic swimmer, did. Born in Florence, she won the FINA Marathon Swimming in 2015, 2016, and 2019. She also pocketed the silver medal in the 2016 Summer Olympics.

MARIO LUZI

Florentine poets in the modern era may be few and far between, but Mario Luzi stands out for his intense verses that describe chaotic transitions. Interestingly, he was influenced by Hermes Trismegistus, an iconic philosopher in the Hellenistic period (post Alexander the Great).

CHIARA FRANCINI

While Florence has had a rich acting past, especially female actors, many of the greats have retired. In the film industry today, nobody represents the acting acumen of the Florentines better than Chiara Francini. She has appeared in several Italian films and television series, showcasing her talent and versatility as an actress. Some of her notable works include "Miracle at St. Anna," "Il Cielo Stellato Fa le Fusa," and "Ti Sposo Ma Non Troppo."

TRANSPORTATION

Florence, being a major cultural and tourist hub in Italy, has a well-developed transportation system that facilitates movement within the city and connections to other parts of Italy and Europe. However, there are a few Limited Traffic Zones (ZTL) in the city where outside vehicles aren't allowed, including in the Historic Center.

BUS

Florence has an extensive network of buses operated by Autolinee Toscane, covering various routes within the city and its outskirts. The C1 - C4 are electric and can off an interesting touch to getting around.

You can buy tickets from the stop itself or from inside the bus, with a validation machine in the front and one in the back.

The morning service is from 6am to 10pm, with the nighttime "Nottetempo" service running from 10pm to 2am.

TRAM

The city has a modern tram system connecting different areas of Florence, including the city center and suburbs. They're a great alternative to avoid traffic, but not a one-stop method to reaching many sights of interest.

Trams run from 5:30pm to midnight, and you can buy tickets at the stations.

TAXI

Taxis are readily available in Florence, and they can be hailed either on the street or found at designated taxi stands. They are a convenient option for traveling within the city, but they can be expensive compared to other modes of transportation.

BICYCLES

Florence's mostly pleasant weather makes it a bike-friendly city with bike lanes and dedicated paths. Many tourists choose to explore the city by bicycle. Rental services and bike-sharing programs are also available.

WALKING

Your own two feet are inarguably the best way to explore the city. The historic center of Florence is relatively compact and crowded, so walking is preferred by most tourists. Many of the main attractions, such as the Uffizi Gallery, the Ponte Vecchio, and the Duomo, are within walking distance of each other.

TRAIN

Florence is well-connected by train services. The main train station, Santa Maria Novella (SMN), serves as a hub for national and international trains, providing easy access to destinations within Italy and beyond, including Rome, Milan, Venice, and other major cities.

CAR RENTAL AND DRIVING

While having a car in Florence might not be necessary due to the city's limited traffic zones and pedestrian-friendly areas, car rental services are available for those wanting to explore the surrounding Tuscan countryside or travel to nearby towns and villages. The ZTL in the city center makes it off-limits to non-resident vehicles during specific hours. Check with your hotel staff or someone local to know when you can commute there in your car.

AIRPORT

The main airport serving Florence is Amerigo Vespucci Airport (FLR), also known as Peretola Airport. It is located around four kilometers from the city center, and it has domestic and a few international flights.

ADDITIONAL RESOURCES

Check out these excellent resources to plan your perfect travel itinerary in Florence:

- www.LonelyPlanet.com, one of the earliest travel guide companies, has some great tips on how to get around Florence.
- Find the finest accommodations in the city on the Europe-based website, www.Booking.com.
- Airbnb has a healthy presence throughout Florence, getting you affordable deals on accommodations.
- Direct links for public transportation, including buses and trams, are found at the Florence Insider.
- Introducing Florence has a comprehensive, well-updated transport guide to browse through.
- Visit Florence has many insightful ideas to plan your trip to the city.
- For readymade, detailed itineraries, visit Headout.com to know when to visit which attraction.

CHAPTER 2

TO AND FROM THE AIRPORT

Now that you have gotten to know Florence, it's time to know how to get there. Which airport do you book the flight ticket for? The answer is simple. There is only one airport in the city: Florence airport, also called Amerigo Vespucci Airport.

There used to be another airport in the early 1900s in the Campo di Marte area, but it wasn't made for commercial flights, only for experimental purposes, and it was shut down in the 1920s.

AMERIGO VESPUCCI AIRPORT

Florence Airport (FLR) is one of the busiest airports in Tuscany, serving over two million passengers per year. [4]

Florence Airport (FLR) is the second-busiest airports in Tuscany, serving over three million passengers per year. It is located in the Peretola neighborhood, in the northwest corner of Florence, no more than 6 kilometers from the city center. It was established in 1931 simply as a large field with no dedicated runways. Planes came and went as they pleased without any restrictions or rules. A few years later, in 1938, the government transformed it into an official airport with runways.

It was extensively used during World War II by both the Italian and German forces. Finally, after the war, commercial flights started operating at the airport. Initially, domestic flights were mainly offered, but as the foot traffic steadily grew in the city, especially from foreign countries, more international flights were added. It was in 1990 when its name was officially changed to Amerigo Vespucci Airport, after the renowned local explorer.

Today, the airport can be reached from all the major Italian cities like Bologna, Rome, Turin, Milan, etc. FLR is also accessible from many other European airports, such as London, Amsterdam, Barcelona, Munich, etc.

It is a world-class airport that has undergone many useful renovations over the past few decades. Before the '90s, there used to be a single pathway for both departures and arrivals. A separate arrivals building was constructed in 1992, followed by a departures section in 1994. A few years later, the runway was extended to allow for better takeoffs, and the terminals and car parking spots were greatly expanded.

GETTING TO AND FROM THE AIRPORT

With only 6 kilometers to the city center, hiring a taxi (cab) or renting a car is the fastest and easiest mode of transport. Browse through the other options, too, if you wish to get an authentic Florentine experience.

TAXI

Taxis are readily available at FLR, waiting outside the arrivals terminal. The journey to the city center takes approximately 10 minutes, depending on traffic. A major benefit of the taxi is for people with a lot of luggage. The paths leading to other modes of transport are cobblestone streets, which will make it difficult to haul huge suitcases. At the time of writing this, taxis have a fixed rate of €22 during daytime and €25.30 after dusk to get to the city center. They will also charge a euro for each piece of luggage.

There usually aren't waiting queues off-season, but if you are visiting during peak times, you may want to book a taxi in advance. Private transfers are readily available, and they provide door-to-door service to your accommodation in Florence. Google "book a taxi from Florence airport," or you can also visit this website to book one directly online: BookTaxi-Florence.com.

TRAM

The tram service is relatively new at FLR. It was established alongside the VolaInBus service in 2019 that operates regularly to and from the city center. The T2 Tram line also connects the airport to the city center (specifically, the Unita stop near the Santa Maria Novella train station). It takes a little longer than road travel because of 12 stops along the route, but the frequency is high, especially during peak hours (about four to five minutes).

A major benefit of the tramway is its cheap price. A one-way ticket costs just €1.50. Large suitcases will require extra tickets, but they still don't go anywhere near the exorbitant prices of taxis. Its only drawback is that you can carry no more than two large suitcases with you. There are clear signs leading to the tram station from the front gate of the airport. Purchase your ticket at an automated machines and validate it at the yellow machines inside the tram.

CAR RENTAL

Various car rental companies operate from the airport if you prefer the flexibility of driving yourself around Florence and its surroundings. A direct, five-minute shuttle service is available to take you to the booking office or the parking lot. First-time travelers won't have much of a problem locating their accommodation on their own, thanks to easy map accessibility on their GPS system. You can also explore alternate scenic routes or grab a bite at a local restaurant along the way.

PROS OF USING AMERIGO VESPUCCI AIRPORT

✦ **Tourist-Friendly Airport**

FLR is not huge, and there are signs leading travelers to their desired destinations at every step, so you won't need anyone's help in getting out through the arrivals terminal.

✦ **Convenient Transportation**

Shuttle service is available to take you from the plane to the arrivals section or from departure to the plane. It will also take you to the parking lot if you have a parked car or are hiring a rental. Getting to the city center is easy via taxis and trams. Private transfers will take you virtually anywhere in Florence from the airport.

+ **Easy Travel to Other Tourist Destinations**

Florence is the nearest city to the airport, but there are many other destinations within reach, too. You can get from the airport to Pisa in an hour (by train, bus, or private transport). The mesmerizing Chianti area in Siena is also an hour's drive away. The extensive rail network of Florence will take you to many other cities in the region.

+ **Accessibility for Disabled Travelers**

The airport is wheelchair-friendly, and there are dedicated private transfer services for the disabled to reach the city center from the airport taxi stand.

The currency exchange terminal is in the arrivals area on the ground floor of the airport. You can also visit C.R. Firenze Bank, situated just two miles away (on your travel route).

CONS OF THE AIRPORT

+ **Limited Direct Flights**

Since there is only one short runway, large planes cannot land at Amerigo Vespucci Airport. That is why there are no direct flights from the U.S. or Canada, or any other long-haul flight. You will have to take a connecting flight from some other place (preferably Pisa or Bologna).

+ **Peak-Hours Traffic**

During the tourist season at peak hours, the traffic between the city center and the airport can be quite exhausting, especially the A11 between the toll booth and the terminal.

ALTERNATE ROUTES

If you don't want to take a connecting flight to Florence airport or wish to avoid the exasperating traffic leading to the city, you can take a few alternate routes that are decidedly scenic and will fill your quota of sightseeing for the day.

FROM PISA

The next nearest airport to Florence is Pisa International Airport, around 98-100km to the west. You can book a direct flight from several U.S. cities to Pisa. Being the largest airport in Tuscany, it is connected to many other parts of the world, too. You can board a high-speed train from the airport bound for Florence, which may cost around €10 and would take about 49 minutes.

A great suggestion would be to take the bus, which costs a little more (around €14), but it's slow enough for you to get to the sights and fast enough to reach Florence in about an hour. Renting a car or a private transfer is the best option, but it may cost you 10 to 20 times more. You can make a number of stops along the way, including Livorno, Volterra, Prato, and Piazza del Duomo.

FROM BOLOGNA

Bologna Guglielmo Marconi Airport is almost the same distance as Pisa, to the north. Taking a train from the airport to Florence is the fastest option, but you won't get to see the sights, even if you are on a slow train, because it passes through many tunnels. It costs €10 to €20 depending on the time of day. Buses are cheaper and travel across several mesmerizing Tuscan terrains, but it will take around 90 minutes to reach your destination. Tunnels are present on roads, too, but there's still enough to see. Rentals and private transfers will cost you a lot more, and they are only recommended if you are already on a road trip.

FROM ROME

This is inarguably the most scenic route to Florence, primarily because it passes through the spellbinding Chianti region. Fiumicino Rome Airport is about 309km to the south of Florence, but if you have time and money on your hands, you can book an exclusive transfer package that will let you admire the beautiful rolling hills of Chianti and taste their elegant wine to your heart's content. It will take you around six hours to reach Florence with services like Prestige Rent and Italy's Best, but it will be an otherworldly experience.

Alternatively, you can take the train, which will reach Florence in two to three hours, depending on its speed. Ticket prices are around €25-35.

CHAPTER 3
RIFREDI

Located in the heart of Florence, Italy, Rifredi attracts travelers with its unique charm and timeless allure. This district, distinguished by its rich history and vibrant character, stands as a testament to the city's cultural legacy. What sets Rifredi apart is not only its architectural marvels but also the sense of authenticity that can be felt so clearly in its cobblestone streets.

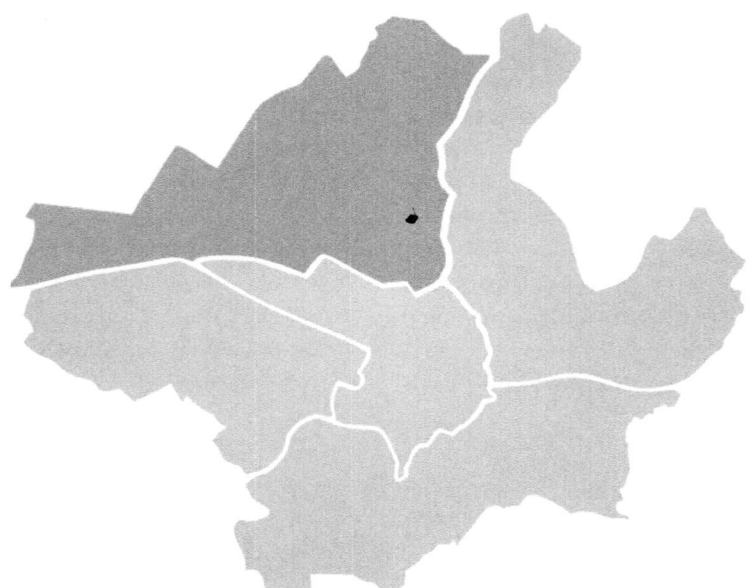

Rifredi. [5]

One cannot help but be captivated by the splendid blend of Renaissance and medieval influences that grace Rifredi, creating the perfect backdrop for exploration. The district has a range of quaint cafes, artisanal boutiques, and hidden gems waiting to be discovered, offering visitors a chance to immerse themselves in the local way of life. You can wander through narrow alleys adorned with ivy-covered facades and find yourself transported to a bygone era where every corner whispers stories of the past.

A must-visit if you're seeking an escape from the bustling city center, Rifridi unveils the quieter side of Florence while still offering so many attractions. Whether you're drawn to historical landmarks and charming squares or simply wish to soak in the authentic Italian atmosphere, Rifredi is a treasure trove waiting to be explored. As you navigate its enchanting streets, you'll find that Rifredi embodies the essence of Florence's timeless beauty, making it a must-visit destination for any traveler eager to uncover the soul of Florence.

HISTORICAL OVERVIEW

Rifredi's roots can be traced back to ancient times, with evidence suggesting human settlements in the area as far back as the Roman era. However, it was during the medieval era that Rifredi began to take shape as a distinct community within the broader framework of Florence. The district was first called "Romito Vittoria" and is the largest district of the city of Florence.

As Florence transitioned into a cultural and economic powerhouse during the Renaissance, Rifredi flourished in tandem. The Medici family, which brought about the city's golden age, was pivotal in shaping Rifredi's destiny. Their influence is etched in the architectural marvels that dot the district, reflecting the luxuriousness and artistic fervor of the Renaissance period.

One of Rifredi's notable landmarks harkens back to the 15th century: the Villa Medicea di Castello. This splendid villa, nestled amid lush gardens, served as a retreat for the Medici family. Over the centuries, it has undergone various transformations, bearing witness to the changing tastes and styles that swept through Florence. Today, the villa remains a testament to the enduring legacy of the Medici dynasty, offering visitors a glimpse into the grand lifestyle of this influential family.

Rifredi's significance expanded during the 19th and early 20th centuries as the district became integral to Florence's industrial and cultural landscape. The establishment of the Rifredi Railway Station in the mid-19th century marked a crucial turning point, connecting the district to the broader railway network and catalyzing economic growth. This period saw the emergence of textile industries and artisan workshops, contributing to Rifredi's reputation as a hub of craftsmanship.

Did You Know?

Rifredi's Resilience: During World War II, Rifredi bore witness to moments of resilience and courage. The local community played a crucial role in supporting resistance efforts, and the district's historic buildings still bear the scars of wartime, telling stories of endurance and solidarity.

The district's historical narrative is also intertwined with the renowned Ospedale Meyer, a pediatric hospital founded in the 1884. Serving as a beacon of healthcare and compassion, the hospital has become an emblematic institution within Rifredi, reflecting the community's commitment to its residents and the broader city.

Despite the passage of time, Rifredi has managed to preserve its distinct character. As Florence continued to expand, Rifredi retained a sense of authenticity and tranquility that set it apart from the bustling city center. Today, its streets are lined with centuries-old buildings adorned with wrought-iron balconies, showcasing the architectural legacy of bygone eras.

Did You Know?

Literary Legacy: Florence served as a source of inspiration for the acclaimed Italian author Vasco Pratolini. His novel, "Le Ragazze di San Frediano," vividly captures the essence of life in Florence during the early 20th century, immortalizing the city's streets and characters in the realm of literature.

MAIN ATTRACTIONS

PIAZZA DALMAZIA

At the historical heart of Rifredi lies the enchanting Piazza Dalmazia, a lively square renowned for its vibrant market and delightful local eateries. Steeped in history, this bustling hub encapsulates the authentic essence of daily life in Florence. The Piazza's market, a kaleidoscope of colors and aromas, attracts locals and visitors alike with a variety of fresh produce, artisanal crafts, and regional delicacies.

What captivates people about Piazza Dalmazia is the intimate connection between vendors and patrons, which shows a sense of community that goes beyond mere transactions. The market is full of culinary delights, with stalls brimming with Tuscan olives, cheeses, and handcrafted pasta.

Located among the market stalls are local eateries where the aroma of freshly brewed espresso mingles with the tantalizing scents of traditional Tuscan dishes. Residents and tourists find comfort in the charming outdoor cafes, where the rhythmic hum of conversation and the clinking of coffee cups create a symphony unique to Piazza Dalmazia.

The authenticity of the Piazza extends beyond its market; it's a gathering place where neighbors exchange pleasantries and visitors immerse themselves in the genuine warmth of Rifredi's community spirit. Locals cherish the square for its role as both a culinary haven and a social nucleus, making Piazza Dalmazia an indispensable gem within the historical fabric of Rifredi.

The Piazza Dalmazia is a lively square renowned for its vibrant market and delightful local eateries. [6]

OSPEDALE MEYER

Founded in the late 19th century, Ospedale Meyer has etched its place in Rifredi's history as a longstanding pediatric hospital. Originally established to address the healthcare needs of orphan children in the community, the hospital has evolved over the years, reflecting the dynamic changes in medical practices and community care.

Ospedale Meyer's historical journey is marked by a commitment to the well-being of the youngest members of Rifredi. Its early days saw the hospital as a response to the pressing health needs of the community, and its growth parallels the advancements in pediatric medicine. The hospital's enduring presence is a testament to its adaptive nature, ensuring it remains a reliable healthcare institution for generations.

While Ospedale Meyer's primary mission is healthcare, it has become more than just a medical facility. Today, visitors come not only for its medical services but also to appreciate the hospital's historical significance and the pivotal role it has played in Rifredi's community life. The hospital's archives and displays offer glimpses into its evolution, showcasing the dedication to pediatric care that has characterized Ospedale Meyer since its inception.

Founded in the late 19th century, Ospedale Meyer has etched its place in Rifredi's history as a longstanding pediatric hospital. [7]

GIARDINO DELL'ORTICOLTURA

Escape the urban hustle and find tranquility in the Giardino dell'Orticoltura. This public garden is a peaceful oasis featuring manicured lawns, blooming flowerbeds, and shaded pathways. It's an ideal spot for a relaxing retreat, offering a quiet respite from the vibrant energy of Rifredi.

As of the writing of this book, regular opening hours are 8:30am to 8pm every day. Please double-check all times before visiting the site.

Escape the urban hustle and find tranquility in the Giardino dell'Orticoltura. [8]

VILLA FABBRICOTTI

Located within a public park, Villa Fabbricotti stands as a splendid 19th-century mansion, inviting visitors to experience the allure of Rifredi's architectural and natural beauty.

Constructed in 1881, Villa Fabbricotti was originally designed as a private residence but has since evolved into a cultural and recreational hub. The mansion's architectural details, characterized by graceful columns and intricate facades, reflect the aesthetic sensibilities of the 19th century.

What makes Villa Fabbricotti a popular destination is not only its architectural significance but also the surrounding public park. The park offers a serene escape from the urban bustle, providing ample green spaces for leisurely strolls, picnics, and moments of relaxation. Towering trees, well-maintained lawns, and meandering pathways create a picturesque setting, making it an ideal spot for both locals and tourists seeking a tranquil retreat.

You can explore the exterior of the mansion, admire its architectural features, and perfectly capture the essence of a bygone era. The park's open spaces can be used for many activities, making it a favored destination for families, couples, and individuals looking to unwind amid the natural beauty of Rifredi.

As of the writing of this book, the site is open from 9:30am to 8pm every day except Saturday and Sunday. Please double-check all operating hours before visiting the site.

Address: Via Vittorio Emanuele II, 64, 50134 Firenze FI, Italy

Villa Fabbricotti was originally designed as a private residence but has since evolved into a cultural and recreational hub. [9]

RIFREDI THEATRE

Rifredi Theater stands out as a vibrant cultural hub, showcasing contemporary performing arts and hosting a variety of cultural events. If you're looking to immerse yourself in the local artistic scene, this venue offers a dynamic and engaging experience.

The theater's diverse calendar features an array of performances, including theatrical productions, concerts, and dance shows. Whether you're a fan of drama, music, or dance, Rifredi Theater provides an opportunity to witness talented artists and performers in action.

As of the writing of this book, the site is open from 4pm to 7pm every day except Sunday. Please double-check all operating hours before visiting the site.

Address: Via Vittorio Emanuele II, 303, 50134 Firenze FI, Italy

Rifredi Theater stands out as a vibrant cultural hub, showcasing contemporary performing arts and hosting a variety of cultural events. [10]

Did You Know?

Rifredi's Musical Heritage: The district has resonated with the melodies of legendary composer Giuseppe Verdi. Rifredi Theatre, founded in 1914, has hosted numerous operatic performances, continuing the tradition of musical excellence that has echoed through the district for generations.

It's a chance to catch a live performance, experience the local arts scene, and perhaps discover emerging talents. One notable event to watch for is the annual Rifredi Arts Festival, a celebration that showcases a diverse range of artistic expressions, including music, dance, and theater.

UNIVERSITY OF FLORENCE'S NOVOLI CAMPUS

Consider a visit to the University of Florence's Novoli Campus, an architectural gem that beautifully blends modernity with Italian design. Located within Rifredi, this campus offers a striking representation of contemporary Italian architecture, marrying functionality with aesthetic appeal.

As you approach the Novoli campus, the standout feature is the sleek facade, adorned with large windows that invite natural light to illuminate the interior spaces. The architects have seamlessly integrated practicality and elegance, creating an environment that fosters both academic pursuits and visual delight.

The exterior landscaping adds to the allure, featuring well-manicured green spaces that provide a serene backdrop to the architectural splendor. From open plazas to thoughtfully designed walkways, every corner of the campus invites exploration and relaxation.

Consider a visit to the University of Florence's Novoli Campus. "

STIBBERT MUSEUM

Stibbert Museum is a house-museum located in the villa on the hill of Montughi. The rooms of the museum are warm and friendly, filled with a sumptuous collection of portraits from different ages. So, if you're looking to experience a journey back in time, this is your go-to museum.

The museum showcases a collection of arms and suits of armor from multiple nations, such as Egypt, India, Germany, and Japan. Today, there are about 50 thousand items.

As of the writing of this book, the site is open from 10am to 6pm on Fridays, Saturdays, and Sundays, 10am to 2pm on Mondays, Tuesdays, and Wednesdays, and is closed on Thursdays. Please double-check all operating hours before visiting the site.

The Stibbert Museum houses about 50 thousand items. [12]

TRANSPORT

To get to the Rifredi district, you can choose from five options, with each taking little to no time and cost.

TRAIN

The most efficient way to go between Rifredi and Florence city center is by train. The journey typically takes around five minutes, depending on the specific train service. Train tickets are reasonably priced, with fares usually ranging from €1 to €3 for a one-way ticket.

BUS

Buses are a convenient option, with lines scattered throughout the district. Lines 76, 28, and 59 are just some that encompass Rifredi. Bus tickets are affordable, averaging around €1.50 for a single journey.

TRAM

Trams offer a comfortable and scenic route. The T2 line cuts through Rifredi and reaches the city center.

TAXI

Taxis provide a quick and door-to-door option, taking around two minutes to reach Rifredi, depending on traffic. Taxi fares vary but generally range from €6 to €8 for the journey.

WALKING

If you prefer a leisurely stroll and wish to explore the city on foot, walking from central Florence to Rifredi takes approximately 45 minutes to one hour. This option allows you to soak in the charm of the city while making your way to the district.

ENTERTAINMENT

RIFREDI THEATRE

Catch a performance at the Rifredi Theatre and enjoy the magic of live performances. Immerse yourself in the cultural richness of Florence, whether through drama, comedy, or more.

CINEMA FLORA

A multiplex of wonder with a wide choice of scheduled shows, Cinema Flora is the best place to unwind while enjoying the big screen. Comfortable seating and family-friendly, it's perfect for an evening out.

Address: Piazza Dalmazia, 2R, 50134 Firenze FI, Italy

WHERE TO EAT

Discover the culinary treasures of Rifredi, where a diverse array of restaurants and cafes beckon with flavors that capture the essence of the district. From traditional Tuscan dishes to international delights, Rifredi's food scene offers something for every palate.

L'ANGLO DEL GUSTO

This charming restaurant is renowned for its authentic Tuscan cuisine. Indulge in a selection of fresh fish, meat, and a wide variety of pizzas cooked in a wood oven. Don't miss the house-made tiramisu for a sweet finish. Visitors rave about the warm ambiance and the chef's commitment to using fresh, local ingredients. The attentive service and extensive wine list also receive high praise.

Address: Via Taddeo Alderotti, 37, 50139 Firenze FI, Italy

LE TRE POSATE

A beloved spot for locals, Le Tre Posate serves up classic Italian comfort food. Their pasta dishes, especially the burrata ravioli with lime and crispy ham, are hailed as favorites. Save room for their delicious, light pistachio panna cotta. People appreciate the homely atmosphere and the welcoming staff. The portion sizes and the quality of the ingredients contribute to a delightful dining experience.

Address: Piazza del Terzolle, 4R, 50127 Firenze FI, Italy

BAR CAFFÈ SMS RIFREDI

This cozy café offers a range of Italian coffee blends and delectable pastries. For an authentic Italian breakfast, try their signature espresso or cappuccino paired with a freshly baked cornetto. Visitors appreciate the café's inviting atmosphere, perfect for a morning coffee or an afternoon break. The friendly baristas and the quality of the coffee receive glowing reviews.

Address: Via Vittorio Emanuele II, 303, 50134 Firenze FI, Italy

Whether you're in the mood for a leisurely Italian meal, a quick coffee break, or a decadent dessert, Rifredi's culinary offerings promise to satisfy your cravings and leave you with a taste of the district's culinary richness.

SHOPPING GUIDE

If you're looking to shop in Rifredi, you will find plenty of local boutiques and markets offering a variety of goods, from artisanal crafts to contemporary fashion. Here's your guide to the must-visit spots for a unique shopping experience in this charming district:

MERCATO DI PIAZZA DALMAZIA

Dive into the vibrant Mercato di Piazza Dalmazia, a bustling market where local vendors showcase fresh produce, cheeses, and handmade goods. Pick up Tuscan olive oil, regional wines, and unique souvenirs. The market's lively atmosphere and the opportunity to interact with local merchants make it a delightful shopping destination. Bargaining is common, adding to the authentic market experience.

Address: Piazza Dalmazia, 50100 Firenze FI, Italy

ANTIQUE TREASURES AT VIA REGINALDO GIULIANI

Explore the antique shops along Via Reginaldo Giuliani for a journey through time. Uncover vintage furniture, retro collectibles, and unique artifacts that tell stories of Rifredi's past. Antique enthusiasts will appreciate the authenticity and character of the items on display. Bargaining is common, providing an opportunity to acquire one-of-a-kind pieces.

ACCOMMODATION

B&B LA PIAZZA

If you're looking for a quiet, scenic place for a romantic getaway or quality-time with your family, B&B La Piazza is the place for you. It is the ultimate location to enjoy a variety of activities, like watching a movie at the Flora Cinema or attending a show at the Rifredi Theatre.

Address: Piazza Dalmazia, n°1, 50141 Firenze FI, Italy

ADELROTTI HOME

Adelrotti Home is the perfect place to stay if you're looking to be surrounded by a lot of beautiful sites. With family rooms, Wi-Fi, and air-conditioning, it's a magnet for couples. Some rooms also have a terrace. It is located about 6km from Piazza della Republica.

Address: Via Taddeo Alderotti, 67, 50139 Firenze FI, Italy

HOTEL RAFFAELLO

Address: Viale Giovanni Battista Morgagni, 19, 50134 Firenze FI, Italy

Exploring Rifredi in Florence unveils a district rich in history, culture, and authentic Italian experiences. From the Renaissance charm of Villa Medicea di Castello to the vibrant local markets, Rifredi offers a captivating journey through time. As you navigate the streets, you'll find a balance between modernity and tradition, epitomized by the University of Florence's Novoli Campus and the halls of the Stibbert Museum. In essence, Rifredi is not just a district; it's a mosaic of experiences waiting to be uncovered.

CHAPTER 4
ISOLOTTO-LEGNAIA

Isolotto-Legnaia is a distinctive district nestled in the western part of Florence, Italy. Known for its local charm and unique character, this neighborhood offers visitors a glimpse into the authentic Florentine lifestyle. From historical landmarks to contemporary attractions, Isolotto-Legnaia provides a diverse range of experiences for those exploring the city.

Isolotto-Legnaia. [13]

BRIEF HISTORICAL BACKGROUND

In the nineteenth century, Isolotto was mainly characterized by numerous industrial settlements but experienced a wide-ranging urban planning project in the twentieth century where an entire social housing district was built on a plan of residential and green spaces with the hopes of developing social aggregation. Legnaia itself was an autonomous commune from 1808 until 1865. As Florence expanded and developed, Islotto-Legnaia transformed into a residential neighborhood while retaining echoes of its industrial past.

Together, Isolotto-Legnaia represents a harmonious blend of history and contemporary life. Visitors can explore the remnants of its rural origins, juxtaposed with modern amenities and cultural offerings that make this district a captivating part of Florence's urban mosaic. From historic landmarks to vibrant community spaces, Isolotto-Legnaia stands as a testament to the city's ability to seamlessly integrate its past with the present.

MAIN ATTRACTIONS

ISOLOTTO MARKET

The Isolotto Market is a contemporary hub that pulsates with the lively energy of local life. Dive into the community vibe as you explore stalls brimming with fresh produce and authentic Italian delicacies. The market is not only a gastronomic delight but also a reflection of the dynamic and diverse spirit of Isolotto-Legnaia. Engage with local artisans, sample regional specialties, and soak in the vibrant atmosphere of this bustling market.

The Isolotto Market is a contemporary hub that pulsates with the lively energy of local life. [14]

VILLA VOGEL AND VILLA STROZZI

Explore the timeless elegance of Renaissance architecture at Villa Vogel and Villa Strozzi. Wander through picturesque gardens and marvel at the historical significance of these well-preserved villas. Each corner tells a story of Florence's aristocratic past, offering visitors a glimpse into the city's cultural heritage amid modern urbanity.

Explore the timeless elegance of Renaissance architecture at Villa Strozzi. [15]

CHIESA DI SANT'ANGELO A LEGNAIA

Chiesa di Sant'Angelo a Legnaia. [16]

Explore the Chiesa di Sant'Angelo a Legnaia, another historic church in the district known for its architectural beauty and religious significance. Admire the intricate details and serene atmosphere as you delve into the spiritual side of Isolotto-Legnaia.

Did You Know?

Did you know that Isolotto-Legnaia was once a predominantly agricultural area with vast fields and orchards? The transformation from its rural origins to a vibrant urban district reflects the dynamic history and adaptability of Florence. Today, as you wander through its streets and parks, you can still catch glimpses of its agrarian past amid the contemporary cultural landscape.

TRANSPORT

Navigating Isolotto-Legnaia is convenient and accessible, with various transportation options ensuring seamless exploration of the district and easy connections to the wider city of Florence.

BUS SERVICES

Isolotto-Legnaia is well-connected to the Florence city center and other neighborhoods through an efficient bus network. Several bus lines, including but not limited to Line 17 and Line 23, provide convenient transportation options. These buses offer a cost-effective and reliable means of reaching key attractions within the district and beyond.

TRAM SERVICES

The tram system in Florence plays a vital role in connecting different parts of the city, and Isolotto-Legnaia benefits from this network. Tram line T2 serves the district, offering a comfortable and scenic route. Trams are a particularly convenient option for traveling to and from the city center, providing a reliable mode of transportation.

BICYCLE RENTALS

Embrace the local lifestyle by exploring Isolotto-Legnaia on two wheels. Bicycle rentals are available in and around the district, allowing visitors to enjoy the scenic routes, including those along the Arno River. Biking is a sustainable and leisurely way to experience the parks, markets, and historical sites in the area.

WALKING

Isolotto-Legnaia is designed for pedestrian exploration, with its picturesque streets and pedestrian-friendly zones. Many attractions, including the Parco Villa Vogel and local markets, are best experienced on foot. Walking not only allows for a more intimate encounter with the surroundings but also provides the opportunity to uncover hidden gems along the way.

TAXI SERVICES AND RIDE-SHARING

Taxis and ride-sharing services are readily available for those seeking a more personalized and convenient mode of transportation. Taxis can be hailed at designated stands while ride-sharing apps provide a modern and flexible alternative for moving around Isolotto-Legnaia and beyond.

CAR RENTALS

While the district is well-suited for walking and public transportation, car rentals are available for those who prefer the flexibility of having their own vehicle. Parking facilities are accessible, and navigating the roads allows visitors to explore nearby attractions at their own pace.

Whether you choose the efficiency of public transportation, the charm of cycling, or the convenience of taxis, Isolotto-Legnaia offers a range of transport options to suit different preferences, ensuring a seamless and enjoyable travel experience.

EXPERIENCES:

GUIDED TOURS OF HISTORIC VILLAS AND GARDENS

Embark on guided tours of the historic villas and gardens, such as Villa Vogel and Villa Strozzi. Explore the Renaissance elegance of these architectural gems while knowledgeable guides share fascinating stories about the aristocratic past and the evolution of Isolotto-Legnaia.

FOOD AND MARKET TOURS

Dive into the gastronomic delights of Isolotto-Legnaia with food and market tours. Explore the Isolotto Market, sampling local produce, cheeses, and traditional Italian delicacies. Engage with passionate vendors, gaining insights into the culinary culture that defines this district.

CULTURAL FESTIVALS AND EVENTS

Keep an eye on the local events calendar for cultural festivals and gatherings in Isolotto-Legnaia. Experience the district coming alive with music, dance, and traditional celebrations, providing an opportunity to engage with the vibrant community spirit.

BIKE TOURS ALONG THE ARNO RIVER

Discover Isolotto-Legnaia and its surroundings on a bike tour. Pedal along the scenic routes bordering the Arno River, exploring the district's parks, landmarks, and charming neighborhoods. Bike tours offer an active and immersive way to experience the unique atmosphere of this Florentine district.

Did You Know?

Did you know that Isolotto-Legnaia hosts an annual community art fair where local artists showcase their creations in the open spaces of Parco delle Cascine? This event not only adds a colorful flair to the district but also reflects the thriving artistic community that calls Isolotto-Legnaia home. Visitors have the chance to engage with artists, purchase unique artworks, and be a part of the vibrant cultural tapestry of this enchanting district.

WHERE TO EAT

TRATTORIA IL BACA

Dive into the flavors of traditional Italian cuisine at Trattoria Il Baca. This welcoming trattoria in the heart of the Legnaia neighborhood serves up classic Tuscan dishes with a focus on fresh, high-quality ingredients. From pasta to seafood, the menu reflects the rich culinary heritage of the region.

Address: Via Simone Martini, 13, 50142 Firenze FI, Italy

PAPPA E CICCIA FIRENZE

Located near the Isolotto Market, Pappa e Ciccia Firenze is a charming family-run pizzeria, offering a wide variety of delicious pizza.

Address: Via Torcicoda, 151R, 50142 Firenze FI, Italy

LA FAMA

Satisfy your sweet tooth at La Fama, a renowned pastry shop near Villa Vogel. Indulge in a tempting array of traditional Italian pastries, cakes, and desserts. Whether you're craving a morning cappuccino and a pastry or a post-dinner treat, La Fama is a delightful choice.

Address: Via Amos Cassioli, 50142 Firenze FI, Italy

LA STREGA NOCCIOLA GELATERIA ARTIGINALE

Conclude your culinary journey with a visit to Gelateria Legnaia. Indulge in artisanal gelato made with high-quality ingredients. Choose from a variety of flavors, each crafted to perfection, and savor a sweet treat as you explore the charming streets of Legnaia.

Address: Via Pisana, 6R, 50143 Firenze FI, Italy

Whether you're seeking traditional Tuscan dishes, international flavors, or a quick bite from a local market, Isolotto-Legnaia offers a diverse culinary scene that caters to every taste and preference.

SHOPPING GUIDE

ISOLOTTO MARKET

Start your shopping adventure at the Isolotto Market, a vibrant hub offering a wide array of fresh produce, local specialties, and artisanal products. From fresh fruits and vegetables to cheeses and handmade crafts, this market captures the essence of the district's community spirit.

Address: Viale delle Magnolie, 8, 50142 Firenze FI, Italy

ARTISAN WORKSHOPS IN LEGNAIA

Explore the charming streets of Legnaia, where you'll find a variety of artisan workshops. From traditional craftsmanship to contemporary art, these workshops showcase the talents of local artisans. Discover uniquely handcrafted items, including ceramics, textiles, and more.

VILLA STROZZI CONCEPT STORE

Visit the Villa Strozzi Concept Store for a curated selection of lifestyle products, home decor, and gifts. This store, located in proximity to Villa Strozzi, combines modern design with traditional influences, offering a unique shopping experience.

LEGNAIA SUNDAY MARKET

If you're visiting on a Sunday, don't miss the Legnaia Sunday Market. This weekly market features a variety of goods, from vintage finds to handmade crafts. It's a great opportunity to mingle with locals and discover unique treasures.

Address: Via Frà Diamante, 12/A, 50143 Firenze FI, Italy

Did You Know?

Did you know that the Isolotto Market hosts occasional events, such as food festivals, where local producers and chefs come together to showcase their culinary expertise? These events not only offer a chance to taste a variety of dishes but also provide insight into the rich gastronomic culture of Isolotto-Legnaia. Keep an eye out for such events in order to immerse yourself in the district's dynamic and flavorful community.

ENTERTAINMENT

LIMONAIA OF VILLA STROZZI

La Limonia is a compelling cultural center with many activities for both children and adults. Walking in its vibrant greenery is a therapeutic experience. You can also go to Piazza del L'Isolotto for fresh produce. If you are someone who likes puzzles, spending the day at the interactive math museum will be a delight.

Address: Via Pisana, 77, 50143 Firenze FI, Italy

GIARDINO DI ARCHIMEDE

Explore mathematics and its applications in a unique way in Il Giardino Di Archimede. Exult yourself in the interactive structure of the museum. Take your kids and let them explore the history of mathematics in a simple, informative, and uncomplicated manner.

Address: Via di S. Bartolo a Cintoia, 19A, 50142 Firenze FI, Italy

Note: As of the writing of this book, the museum is temporarily closed, so double-check before visiting the site.

LIVE PERFORMANCES AT TEATRO CANTIERE FLORIDA

Teatro Cantiere Florida is a cultural space that hosts live performances, including theater, music, and dance. Check the schedule for upcoming events and immerse yourself in the local arts scene within this intimate venue.

Address: Via Pisana, 111/R, 50143 Firenze FI, Italy

VILLA VOGEL PARK

Rejoice in Villa Vogel Park's beauty by taking a stroll in its verdure. This park is family-friendly, with a playground and a roller skating rink. There are also several performances for children. The abundance of trees there is the perfect reason for you to enjoy a picnic on a sunny summer day.

Address: Via A. Canova, 72, 50142 Firenze FI, Italy

CULTURAL FESTIVALS IN LEGNAIA

Stay tuned for cultural festivals and events in the Legnaia neighborhood. These gatherings often feature live performances, art installations, and activities that bring the community together. Join in the festivities to witness the lively and celebratory spirit of Isolotto-Legnaia.

Whether it's live performances, cultural festivals, or outdoor activities, Isolotto-Legnaia offers a variety of entertainment options that cater to different tastes and interests. Be sure to check local event calendars and embrace the lively and creative atmosphere of this dynamic Florentine district.

ACCOMMODATIONS

BED AND BREAKFAST LA TAVERNETTA

Enjoy a cozy and personalized stay at Bed and Breakfast La Tavernetta. This accommodation option offers a warm ambiance and a delicious breakfast to kick-start your day. Experience the hospitality of local hosts who can provide insights into the best of Isolotto-Legnaia.

Address: Via Pio Fedi, 53, 50142 Firenze FI, Italy

AIRBNB OPTIONS

Explore the diverse range of Airbnb options available in Isolotto-Legnaia. From stylish apartments to quaint houses, Airbnb provides a chance to experience the district like a local. Choose accommodations that suit your preferences and enjoy a personalized stay.

ALEX FLORENCE

This hotel is an excellent option for you if you want a lower budget option that's still close to the city. Alex Florence features high ceilings with traditionally decorated rooms. It is also a close walk to the tram stop and a five kilometer walk to Parco delle Cascine.

Address: Via Baccio da Montelupo, 18, 50142 Firenze FI, Italy

AGRITURISMO NEAR ISOLOTTO

Experience a unique stay at an agriturismo near Isolotto. These farm stays provide a blend of rural charm and modern comforts. Enjoy the tranquility of the countryside while being within reach of Isolotto-Legnaia's attractions.

Did You Know?

Did you know that some accommodations in Isolotto-Legnaia offer special packages or guided experiences that include local tours, cooking classes, or access to cultural events? When planning your stay, inquire about any unique offering that could enhance your experience and provide a deeper connection to the district and its community.

CHAPTER 5
CAMPO DI MARTE

Campo di Marte is a lively district situated in the northeast part of the historic city center of Florence, Italy. Renowned for its energetic atmosphere, diverse recreational facilities, and vibrant local life, Campo di Marte offers a unique blend of historical charm and modern vitality. The district provides a dynamic contrast to the more traditional neighborhoods of Florence, attracting both residents and visitors seeking a lively urban experience.

Campo di Marte. [17]

HISTORICAL BACKGROUND

Historically, Campo di Marte was originally conceived in the 19th century as a project by Luigi de Cambray Digny. This area served as a training ground for the military, reflecting its original purpose as a space for martial exercises and tournaments. Over time, the district evolved from its military origins into a thriving urban center, experiencing significant development during the late 19th and early 20th centuries.

During this period, Campo di Marte witnessed the expansion of the city beyond its medieval walls, leading to the establishment of new neighborhoods and infrastructure. The district became a hub for residential and commercial activities, attracting a diverse population and contributing to its present-day character as a bustling and cosmopolitan part of Florence.

Today, Campo di Marte retains traces of its historical significance, with architectural remnants and landmarks that harken back to its military past. As Florence's urban landscape continued to transform, the district embraced modernity, incorporating contemporary amenities, parks, and cultural spaces. Campo di Marte stands as a testament to Florence's ability to seamlessly blend its rich history with the evolving needs of a dynamic and growing city.

MAIN ATTRACTIONS

FOOTBALL MUSEUM OF COVERCIANO

If you're a football fan, you cannot miss the chance to visit the Football Museum of Coverciano. The museum includes a comprehensive collection of trophies won over the years, such as the World Championships of 1934, 1938, and 1982.

Take delight in walking through Italy's history. From its display of jerseys, balls, and trophies, you will find a story to tell to your friends back home.

The museum is located on Viale Palazzeschi and is owned by the Football Museum Foundation.

As of the writing of this book, operating hours are 10am to 6pm every day. Double-check all times before visiting the site.

Address: Viale Aldo Palazzeschi, 20, 50135 Firenze FI, Italy

Don't miss out on visiting the football museum. [18]

ARTEMIO FRANCHI STADIUM

Despite the many changes made over the years, Artemio Franchi Stadium remains one of the most important stadiums in Italy. A lot of significant matches were played in it, and it's home to the great ACF Fiorentina. Not to mention, it's been the venue for some great concerts like David Bowie and Madonna.

Football fans love it, and if you're one of them, you can't miss the chance to experience such electric energy. Everyone who visited it said they had a terrific experience!

Address: Viale Manfredo Fanti, 4, 50137 Firenze FI, Italy

The Artemio Franchi Stadium, home to ACF Fiorentina. [19]

THE ENZO PAZZAGLI ART PARK

If you're an art-enthusiast, The Enzo Pazzagli Art Park is the place to go. Delve into the beauty of the artworks by artists like Enzo Pazzagli, Sauro Cavallini, and Marcello Guasti.

The park is located in the east of Florence. It is a large garden containing more than 200 works of art. There are also several art workshops, making it an ideal school trip for children. What is amazing about this park is that at night, the artworks are illuminated.

As of the writing of this book, normal operating hours are 12pm to 7pm on Saturdays and Sundays, and the park is closed for the rest of the week. Double-check the times before visiting this site.

Address: Via Sant'Andrea a Rovezzano, 5, 50136 Firenze FI, Italy

CHURCH OF SAN MICHELE IN SAN SALVI

The Church of San Michele in San Salvi is located in the Coverciano neighborhood of Florence and was built in the 11th century by the Vallombrosans. Although it was partially destroyed in the 1500s, it was rebuilt to offer those who visit it a breathtaking experience.

The church contains The Last Supper by Andrea Del Sarto, which took almost 8 years to be created.

Address: Piazza di S. Salvi, 10, 50135 Firenze FI, Italy

VIALE DEI MILLE

Take a leisurely stroll along Viale dei Mille, a charming avenue lined with shops and cafes, and a glimpse into everyday Florentine life. Immerse yourself in the local atmosphere, discover boutiques, and enjoy a cup of coffee or gelato in one of the inviting cafes that dot this lively thoroughfare.

Take a leisurely stroll along Viale dei Mille. [20]

Did You Know?

Did you know that Campo di Marte was named after the Campus Martius, a large public area in ancient Rome dedicated to Mars, the Roman god of war? While the district's history is rooted in military training grounds, it has transformed into a vibrant and dynamic part of Florence, embracing sports, culture, and a lively community spirit. The juxtaposition of its historical origins with modern life reflects the district's unique character.

NELSON MANDELA FORUM

The Nelson Mandela Forum is an indoor sports arena that hosts a lot of fun events, including sports events, concerts, films and shows, political congresses, and different kinds of exhibitions. Its unique stage makes it a wonderful experience to have while in Florence.

It is located in the Campo di Marte area, near the Artemio Franchi Stadium. Depending on the events happening at the time, the entrance fees are decided.

As of the writing of this book, normal operating hours are:

Monday, Wednesday and Friday – 8am to 9pm

Tuesday and Thursday – 8am to 10pm

Saturday – 8am to 2pm

Sunday - closed

Double-check the times before visiting this site.

Address: Piazza Enrico Berlinguer, 1, 50137 Firenze FI, Italy

TRANSPORTATION

Campo di Marte is well-connected, providing convenient transportation options for residents and visitors to explore the district and beyond.

TRAIN STATION CAMPO DI MARTE

The Campo di Marte train station serves as a major transportation hub, connecting the district to other parts of Florence and Italy. Located northeast of the city center, this train station facilitates easy access to nearby attractions and offers a convenient mode of transportation for those exploring the region.

BUS SERVICES

Campo di Marte is served by various bus lines, offering efficient and affordable transportation within the district and connecting it to different neighborhoods in Florence. Lines 11, 17, and 7 are just a few. Bus stops are strategically located, providing accessibility to key attractions, shopping areas, and cultural venues.

BICYCLE RENTALS

Embrace the bicycle-friendly atmosphere of Campo di Marte by renting a bike. Many rental shops in the district provide an eco-friendly and enjoyable way to explore the area and nearby attractions. Cycling along the tree-lined streets and avenues is a popular choice for both locals and visitors.

TAXI SERVICES AND RIDE-SHARING

Taxis are readily available in Campo di Marte, offering a convenient mode of transportation, especially for those who prefer a more personalized and direct option. Additionally, ride-sharing services operate in the area, providing flexibility and ease of travel.

WALKING

Given its relatively compact size and pedestrian-friendly infrastructure, Campo di Marte is ideal for exploring on foot. A leisurely stroll along the streets allows visitors to absorb the local atmosphere and discover hidden gems.

CAR RENTALS

While not essential for navigating Campo di Marte, car rentals can be considered for those planning to explore the surrounding areas or venture into the Tuscan countryside. Rental agencies are available, and parking facilities can be found throughout the district.

Whether you choose the efficiency of public transportation, the flexibility of cycling, or the convenience of taxis, Campo di Marte offers a range of transport options to suit different preferences, allowing you to explore the district and beyond with ease. Unfortunately, the tram lines do not run through this district, but the bus lines and train should get you where you want to go.

ENTERTAINMENT

Campo di Marte offers a diverse array of entertainment options, ensuring that visitors and residents can enjoy a vibrant cultural and recreational scene in the district:

LIVE EVENTS AT NELSON MANDELA FORUM

The Nelson Mandela Forum is a versatile venue hosting live events, including concerts, sports competitions, and cultural performances. Check the schedule for upcoming shows, as this venue contributes to the lively entertainment scene in Campo di Marte.

STADIO ARTEMIO FRANCHI ATMOSPHERE

Immerse yourself in the electric atmosphere of Stadio Artemio Franchi during ACF Fiorentina's home games. Whether you're a football enthusiast or not, attending a match allows you to experience the passion and energy of Florence's sports scene.

COMBO SOCIAL CLUB

For nightlife lovers, Combo Social Club is a great attraction for young adults looking to have some fun. This nightclub offers different kinds of music to dance to, from commercial to underground to hip-hop.

It is also a place that hosts concerts for different genres. So, if you're looking for a great night out with your friends, Combo Social Club is the place to go. With its illuminating disco ball on the dance floor, it will be a night you will never forget!

Address: Via Mannelli, 2, 50136 Firenze FI, Italy

CULTURAL EXHIBITIONS AND WORKSHOPS

Explore cultural exhibitions and workshops held in community spaces and galleries in Campo di Marte. These events often showcase the work of local artists, fostering a sense of creativity and community engagement.

RELAXATION AT VIALE DEI MILLE CAFES

Enjoy the entertainment of everyday Florentine life by spending leisurely hours at the cafes along Viale dei Mille. Sip on a cappuccino, people-watch, and soak in the vibrant atmosphere of this bustling avenue.

Whether it's live performances, sports events, or cultural gatherings, Campo di Marte provides a diverse range of entertainment options that cater to different tastes and interests. Check local event calendars to stay updated on the dynamic and lively entertainment scene in this Florentine district.

EXPERIENCES

CULINARY EXPLORATION ALONG VIALE DEI MILLE

Embark on a culinary adventure along Viale dei Mille, sampling the diverse offerings of local cafes, shops, and eateries. Consider joining food tours or thematic tastings that highlight Tuscan cuisine and the unique flavors of Campo di Marte. This experience allows you to savor the culinary delights while immersing yourself in the local culture.

ART AND CULTURAL EVENTS

Stay informed about art exhibitions, cultural festivals, and events taking place in Campo di Marte. Galleries, community spaces, and cultural institutions often host thematic events, providing an opportunity to engage with local art, music, and creativity.

BIKE TOURS AND OUTDOOR ADVENTURES

Explore Campo di Marte and its surroundings on a bike tour. Guided tours can take you through the district's streets, parks, and nearby landmarks, offering a dynamic and active way to experience the vibrant atmosphere of this Florentine neighborhood.

WHERE TO EAT

Campo di Marte boasts a diverse culinary scene, offering a range of dining options from traditional Tuscan fare to international cuisine. Here are some notable places to eat in the district.

RUGBIER BIERSTUBE

Rugbier Bierstube is a casual dining spot with a view of rugby grounds. This relaxed restaurant serves excellent Italian-German fusion food and offers a selection of craft beers.

Address: Viale Pasquale Paoli, 21, 50137 Firenze FI, Italy

COTTA A PUNTINO PIZZERIA RISTORANTE

Cotta a Puntino Pizzeria Ristorante is a well-known Italian restaurant in Campo di Marte. They offer a wide variety of pizzas as well as authentic Italian appetizers, main courses, and desserts.

Address: Via Guido Biagi, 6/8 Rosso, 50135 Firenze FI, Italy

L'ANGOLO DEL MARE

L'angolo del mare is a seafood-focused restaurant that combines fresh ingredients with a creative flair. With a menu showcasing a variety of fish dishes, it's a great choice for those seeking a taste of the Mediterranean in the heart of Florence.

Address: Viale Edmondo de Amicis, 1, 50137 Firenze FI, Italy

PASTICCERIA STEFANIA

Pasticceria Stefania is a delightful bakery where you can indulge in a variety of pastries, cakes, and sweet treats. Whether you're craving a morning cappuccino and a pastry or an afternoon dessert, this charming spot offers a delectable selection.

Address: Viale Edmondo de Amicis, 1, 50137 Firenze FI, Italy

GELATERIA PASTICCERIA BADIANI

For a refreshing treat, visit Gelateria Pasticceria Badiani. Indulge in a wide array of flavors made with high-quality ingredients, and experience the authentic taste of Italian gelato.

Address: Viale dei Mille, 20/r, 50131 Firenze FI, Italy

Whether you're in the mood for traditional Tuscan dishes, fresh seafood, or delectable pastries, Campo di Marte provides a range of dining options to suit every palate and occasion.

SHOPPING GUIDE

Campo di Marte offers a mix of shopping experiences, from boutiques and concept stores to local markets. Here's a guide to exploring the district's diverse shopping scene:

VIALE DEI MILLE BOUTIQUES

Stroll along Viale dei Mille; the lively avenue in Campo di Marte is lined with boutiques and shops. Explore fashion boutiques, accessory stores, and charming shops offering a variety of goods. From trendy clothing to unique accessories, Viale dei Mille caters to diverse tastes.

LA BOTTEGA ITALIANA DI FIRENZE

La Bottega Italiana di Firenze is a market that emphasizes local and sustainable products. Here, you can find fresh produce, artisanal foods, and handmade crafts. It's an ideal place to discover unique items while supporting local farmers and producers.

Address: Via Lungo l'Affrico, 172, 50137 Firenze FI, Italy

CONCEPT STORE AT NELSON MANDELA FORUM

Explore the concept store at the Nelson Mandela Forum, which often features a curated selection of sports-related merchandise, apparel, and memorabilia. It's an excellent place for sports enthusiasts to find unique items and souvenirs.

Address: Piazza Enrico Berlinguer, 1, 50137 Firenze FI, Italy

ACCOMMODATIONS

Campo di Marte offers a variety of accommodations, ranging from charming guesthouses to modern hotels, providing visitors with comfortable options to suit their preferences and travel styles.

VILLA STROZZI RESIDENCE

Experience the charm of a guesthouse stay at Villa Strozzi Residence. Located near Villa Strozzi, this accommodation option combines historic elegance with modern comforts. Enjoy personalized service and a unique atmosphere in this carefully restored residence.

Address: Via Madonna delle Grazie, 18, 50135 Firenze FI, Italy

HOSTEL 7 SANTI

Hostel 7 Santi is a welcoming and centrally-located accommodation option in Campo di Marte that occupies a former 19th century convent. This hostel offers mixed and female-only dorms with shared or en suite bathrooms and has multiple communal areas. From this hostel, you can take a 3-minute walk to Artemio Franchi stadium and it is only a 9-minute walk to Firenze Campo di Marte train station.

Address: Viale dei Mille, 11, 50131 Firenze FI, Italy

PALAZZO LOMBARDO AFFITTACAMERE

Palazzo Lombardo Affittacamere is a posh guesthouse offering a luxurious atmosphere in Campo di Marte. With personalized service and well-appointed rooms, it provides a comfortable retreat for travelers seeking a more intimate lodging experience.

Address: Viale dei Mille, 6, 50131 Firenze FI, Italy

HOTEL DELLA ROBBIA

Hotel Della Robbia is a stylish and modern hotel in the heart of Campo di Marte. Featuring contemporary design and amenities, it offers a comfortable and convenient stay for travelers exploring the district and nearby areas.

Address: Via dei della Robbia, 7, 50132 Firenze FI, Italy

B&B MARTINI

B&B Martini provides a charming and familial atmosphere for guests. With cozy rooms and a hearty breakfast, this bed and breakfast is an excellent choice for those seeking a more personal touch in their accommodation.

Address: Via Vittorio Fossombroni, 6, 50136 Firenze FI, Italy

HOTEL MERIDIANA

Hotel Meridiana is located towards the edge of Campo di Marte, however it is a close walk to the train station and many of the attractions. This hotel features functional rooms with warm décor and has a restaurant and a bar.

Address: Viale Don Giovanni Minzoni, 25, 50129 Firenze FI, Italy

VILLA NEROLI

Villa Neroli is a 4-star hotel with a charming architecture and stylish feel. Additionally, it offers spacious, comfortable rooms with a gorgeous view of the garden. The hotel is only a few minutes from the Artemio Franchi stadium and the Mandela Forum.

Address: Via Gabriele D'Annunzio, 141a, 50135 Firenze FI, Italy

Did You Know?

Did you know that some accommodations in Campo di Marte offer special packages or guided experiences that include local tours, cooking classes, or access to cultural events? When planning your stay, inquire about any unique offerings that can enhance your experience and provide a deeper connection to the district and its community.

CHAPTER 6
Centro Storico

Centro Storico, also known as the heart and soul of Florence, is where history, art, and culture intertwine to showcase Italian heritage. Nestled along the banks of the Arno River, this UNESCO World Heritage Site is a living testament to the Renaissance era and is filled with architectural wonders.

Centro Storico. [21]

Centro Storico, literally translating to "historic center," is a labyrinthine maze of narrow cobblestone streets, bustling piazzas, and majestic landmarks. As you wander through its enchanting alleys, you'll find yourself immersed in the timeless charm of Florence, with its well-preserved medieval and Renaissance architecture that whispers tales of a bygone era.

What truly sets Centro Storico apart is its unrivaled collection of art and history. The famed Uffizi Gallery, home to masterpieces by Botticelli, Leonardo da Vinci, and Michelangelo, is a testament to the city's artistic prowess. The iconic Florence Cathedral, with its majestic dome designed by Brunelleschi, dominates the skyline and invites visitors to marvel at its architectural splendor.

While history echoes through every corner, Centro Storico is also a vibrant hub of modern life. Local markets, like the Mercato Centrale, beckon with the aroma of fresh produce and regional delicacies. Cafés and trattorias line the streets, offering a taste of Tuscan cuisine that's sure to delight the senses.

As you explore Centro Storico, you'll get to cross the Ponte Vecchio, a medieval bridge adorned with charming shops, and soak in the panoramic views of the city from the Piazzale Michelangelo. Whether you're an art enthusiast, a history buff, or simply a traveler in search of authentic experiences, Centro Storico promises an unforgettable journey through the heart of Florence, where the past and present seamlessly blend to create an enchanting destination like no other.

HISTORICAL BACKGROUND

The roots of Centro Storico can be traced back to Roman times when Florence, known as Florentia, was established as a settlement for retired Roman soldiers. However, it was during the medieval period that the city truly began to flourish.

By the 14th century, Florence had evolved into a thriving mercantile and banking center, with powerful families like the Medici shaping its destiny. These influential patrons of the arts played a pivotal role in transforming Florence into the epicenter of the Renaissance, a cultural and intellectual movement that revolutionized art, science, and philosophy.

The heart of Centro Storico showcases the architectural achievements of this era, with landmarks like the Florence Cathedral, also known as the Duomo, and the Baptistery of St. John standing as iconic symbols of Renaissance brilliance. The construction of the cathedral, with its groundbreaking dome designed by Filippo Brunelleschi, marked a monumental achievement in engineering and aesthetics.

The Uffizi Gallery, located in the heart of Centro Storico, was originally built as government offices for the Medici family. Over time, it evolved into one of the world's premier art museums, housing masterpieces by renowned artists such as Botticelli, Leonardo da Vinci, and Raphael.

Centro Storico also played a central role in the political turmoil that characterized Florence during the Renaissance. The Palazzo Vecchio, situated in the Piazza della Signoria, served as the city's political hub and witnessed the rise and fall of various rulers and regimes. The imposing fortress-like structure stands as a symbol of the city's political history and power struggles.

Despite the challenges of war, political strife, and social upheavals, Centro Storico has managed to preserve its medieval and Renaissance charm. The meticulous preservation of its historic buildings, narrow streets, and grandiose squares allows visitors to step back in time and immerse themselves in the captivating narrative of Florence's evolution.

Did You Know?

Centro Storico is often referred to as the "Cradle of the Renaissance." This transformative cultural movement, which spanned the 14th to 17th centuries, found its epicenter in Florence. The Medici family, prominent patrons of the arts, played a pivotal role in fostering this period of great intellectual and artistic advancement. The legacy of the Renaissance is vividly displayed in the masterpieces that grace the Uffizi Gallery and the architectural marvels scattered throughout the district.

MAIN ATTRACTIONS

THE DUOMO

Make sure to visit the awe-inspiring Florence Cathedral, commonly known as the Duomo, situated in the heart of Centro Storico. This monumental architectural marvel showcases the city's artistic prowess during the Renaissance. The crowning jewel of the Duomo is its magnificent dome, a masterpiece designed by Filippo Brunelleschi. Standing proudly as the largest brick dome ever constructed, it offers an unparalleled view of Florence if you manage to climb its narrow staircase.

As you explore the cathedral, take a look at the intricate façade adorned with delicate red, green, and white marble panels, showcasing work by some of the greatest Tuscan artists. The Bell Tower, designed by Giotto, adds another layer of elegance to the ensemble. A visit to the Duomo is an immersion into the architectural splendors of Florence, an experience that will leave you with a profound appreciation for the city's artistic and engineering achievements.

As of the writing of this book, normal operating hours are 10:15am to 3:45pm every day except Sundays when it is closed. Double-check all times before visiting this site.

Address: Piazza del Duomo, 50122 Firenze FI, Italy

The Duomo is an architectural marvel that showcases the city's artistic prowess during the Renaissance. [22]

Did You Know?

As you admire the stunning bronze doors of the Baptistery of St. John, take note of the intricate relief sculptures. Lorenzo Ghiberti's masterful "Gates of Paradise" depicts biblical scenes with a level of detail that captivates viewers. Interestingly, Michelangelo dubbed them the "Gates of Paradise" for their unparalleled beauty. The gilded doors are adorned with symbolic elements and biblical stories, providing a visual narrative that adds layers of meaning to this iconic structure.

UFFIZI GALLERY

Step into a world-class museum that unfolds the rich tapestry of Renaissance art – the Uffizi Gallery. Housed in a magnificent 16th-century palace, this cultural gem boasts an unparalleled collection of masterpieces by some of the greatest artists in history. As you wander through the expansive halls, you'll encounter works by Botticelli, Michelangelo, Raphael, and Leonardo da Vinci. Stand in awe before Botticelli's ethereal "The Birth of Venus" and "Primavera" and witness the raw power of Michelangelo's "Holy Family."

The Uffizi Gallery will take you on a chronological journey through the Renaissance period, revealing the evolution of artistic techniques and styles. The opulent ceilings, adorned with intricate frescoes, add to the gallery's grandeur. For art enthusiasts, the Uffizi Gallery is not merely a collection of paintings but a pilgrimage to the very heart of Renaissance creativity, where each brushstroke narrates the story of a cultural revolution.

As of the writing of this book, normal operating hours are 8:15am to 6:30pm every day except Mondays when it is closed and Tuesdays when it is open until 9:30pm. Double-check all times before visiting this site.

Address: Piazzale degli Uffizi, 6, 50122 Firenze FI, Italy

The Uffizi Gallery will take you on a chronological journey through the Renaissance period. [23]

THE PONTE VECCHIO

Crossing the Arno River via the Ponte Vecchio is not just a journey from one side of Florence to the other; it's a stroll through centuries of history and craftsmanship. As you walk this iconic bridge, the atmosphere is alive with the echoes of the past. The Ponte Vecchio has been home to goldsmiths and jewelers since the 16th century, and today, it stands as a living testament to Florence's artisanal heritage.

You can gaze at the glittering jewelry displays in the historic shops that line the bridge; each piece is crafted with meticulous attention to detail. The Vasari Corridor, a hidden passage for the Medici family, runs above the shops, adding an air of mystery to the ambiance. Make sure that you take a moment to absorb the views of the Arno River, framed by the bridge's medieval arches. The Ponte Vecchio is not merely a crossing; it's a historic shopping experience that immerses visitors in the city's enduring tradition of craftsmanship.

Address: Ponte Vecchio, 50125 Firenze FI, Italy

As you walk this iconic bridge, the atmosphere is alive with the echoes of the past. 24

Did You Know?

Beneath the grand halls and opulent rooms of Palazzo Vecchio lie a network of secret passages and hidden chambers. Built for strategic escapes and clandestine meetings during times of political turmoil, these concealed spaces offer a glimpse into the intrigue and conspiracies that once permeated the corridors of power in Renaissance Florence. While some passages are open to the public, others remain shrouded in mystery, preserving the palace's enigmatic allure.

PALAZZO VECCHIO

Palazzo Vecchio, anchoring the Piazza della Signoria, is more than a town hall; it's Florence's political and historical evolution. The Salone dei Cinquecento, a luxurious hall adorned with monumental frescoes by Giorgio Vasari, serves as a grand stage for the city's eventful past. When standing beneath the vaulted ceilings, imagine the political gatherings and events that shaped the course of Florentine history.

The Arnolfo Tower, an imposing medieval structure, provides panoramic views of Florence, revealing the city's layout as it unfolds beneath you. Explore the hidden passages and chambers within Palazzo Vecchio, delving further into the secrets of Medici intrigue and political maneuvering. The palace is a living archive where each stone tells a different chapter in the history of the city, rather than being just a museum.

As of the writing of this book, normal operating hours are 9am to 7pm every day except Thursday when the site closes at 2pm. Double-check all times before visiting this site.

Address: P.za della Signoria, 50122 Firenze FI, Italy

Palazzo Vecchio, anchoring the Piazza della Signoria, is more than a town hall; it's Florence's political and historical evolution. [25]

THE PIAZZA DELLA SIGNORIA

The Piazza della Signoria isn't just a square; it's an open-air sculpture gallery where history and art converge. Surrounded by iconic landmarks, this vibrant public space is filled with remarkable sculptures that tell tales of heroism, mythology, and political allegory. Gaze upon the awe-inspiring replica of Michelangelo's David, standing proudly at the entrance of the Palazzo Vecchio. Marvel at the bronze brilliance of Cellini's "Perseus with the Head of Medusa" and ponder the allegorical messages embedded in the Neptune Fountain.

The Loggia dei Lanzi, an open-air gallery, houses a captivating collection of Renaissance sculptures, each one a masterpiece in its own right. Whether you're an art enthusiast or simply seeking the lively ambiance of a bustling square, Piazza della Signoria offers a multifaceted experience that encapsulates the essence of Florence's cultural richness.

The Piazza della Signoria isn't just a square; it's an open-air sculpture gallery where history and art converge. [26]

THE ACCADEMIA GALLERY

The Accademia Gallery is a sanctuary for art lovers, providing an intimate encounter with one of the greatest sculptures in history – Michelangelo's David. As you enter the gallery, your gaze will be drawn to the colossal figure, standing with unparalleled grace and precision. Michelangelo's attention to anatomical detail and the sheer mastery of his craftsmanship become evident as you circle the statue. Beyond David, the Accademia's halls house an impressive array of Renaissance art, including works by Botticelli, Ghirlandaio, and Allori.

The immersive experience goes beyond observing; it's about feeling the energy and creativity that define Florentine artistry. The Accademia Gallery invites visitors to experience a pilgrimage instead of just being a destination, allowing them to be in David's presence and observe the creative development that influenced Renaissance Florence's cultural environment.

As of the writing of this book, normal operating hours are 8:15am to 6:20pm every day except Mondays when it is closed. Double-check all times before visiting this site.

Address: Via Ricasoli, 58/60, 50129 Firenze FI, Italy

The Accademia Gallery is a sanctuary for art lovers. [27]

Did You Know?

The renowned poet Dante Alighieri, author of the epic "Divine Comedy," was born and raised in Florence. Although his birthplace is not precisely known, it is widely believed to be in the heart of Centro Storico. Dante's literary contributions had a profound impact on the Italian language, and his legacy is celebrated throughout the district. Keep an eye out for tributes to this literary giant as you explore the historic streets.

PIAZZALE MICHELANGELO

Piazzale Michelangelo is a panoramic terrace situated on a hill south of the Arno River. It offers one of the most breathtaking views of Florence, featuring the iconic landmarks of the city. Visitors can enjoy the open space, adorned with copies of Michelangelo's sculptures, and revel in the beauty of the Florence skyline.

Address: Piazzale Michelangelo, 50125 Firenze FI, Italy

Piazzale Michelangelo is a panoramic terrace situated on a hill south of the Arno River. [28]

BASILICA DI SAN MINIATO AL MONTE

Perched on a hill overlooking Florence, the Basilica di San Miniato al Monte is a stunning example of Romanesque architecture. Constructed between the 11th and 13th centuries, its exterior is adorned with a captivating green-and-white marble facade. Inside, visitors are treated to a mesmerizing display of frescoes, mosaics, and intricate details. The cemetery adjacent to the basilica, the Cemetery of Porto Sante, offers a peaceful retreat and boasts breathtaking views of Florence.

As of the writing of this book, the opening hours are 9:30am to 1pm and then 3:30pm to 7pm every day. Please double-check all times before visiting the site.

Address: Via delle Porte Sante, 34, 50125 Firenze FI, Italy

The Basilica di San Miniato al Monte is a stunning example of Romanesque architecture. [29]

TEATRO PUCCINI

The Teatro Puccini stands as a cultural gem, hosting a diverse array of performances. From captivating plays to soul-stirring concerts, this historic theater invites art enthusiasts to immerse themselves in Florence's vibrant cultural scene. The intimate setting of Teatro Puccini creates a unique atmosphere, allowing visitors to unforgettably connect with the city's artistic heritage.

Address: Via delle Cascine, 41, 50144 Firenze FI, Italy

The Teatro Puccini stands as a cultural gem, hosting a diverse array of performances. [30]

THE VASARI CORRIDOR

Embark on a journey through time and exclusivity as you explore the Vasari Corridor, an elevated passageway that whispers secrets from the Medici era. Commissioned by the Grand Duke Cosimo I in the 16th century, this corridor served as a private route connecting the Uffizi Gallery to the Pitti Palace, allowing the Medici rulers to move discreetly between their administrative offices and residences.

Today, a section of the corridor is open to the public, offering a rare glimpse into the hidden corners of Florence. Filled with self-portraits and an extensive collection of art, the Vasari Corridor showcases the Medici's influence on the city's cultural and political landscape. As you look at this architectural marvel, high above the bustling streets, you will not only explore hidden corners of Florence but also gain insight into the luxury and intrigue that defined the Medici era.

Address: Lungarno degli Archibusieri, 50122 Firenze FI, Italy

The Vasari Corridor is an elevated passageway that whispers secrets from the Medici era. [31]

PARCO DELLE CASCINE

Parco delle Cascine, Florence's largest public park, sprawls along the serene banks of the Arno River. Its expansive green spaces provide an ideal setting for picnics, sports activities, and leisurely walks. Dive into the tranquility of nature while discovering historical monuments dotted throughout the park. The Parco delle Cascine is a cherished retreat for locals and the perfect spot to unwind amid the beauty of Florence's outdoors.

Address: Piazzale delle Cascine, 50144 Firenze FI, Italy

Parco delle Cascine, Florence's largest public park, sprawls along the serene banks of the Arno River. [32]

CHURCH OF SANTA MARIA DEL FIORE

The Church of Santa Maria del Fiore is an iconic attraction. Known for its impressive facade and historical significance, the cathedral is a must-visit. Marvel at the intricate details of the architecture and learn about the religious and cultural heritage tied to this renowned landmark.

As of the writing of this book, the site is open from 10:15am to 3:45pm every day except Sunday. Please double-check all operating hours before visiting the site.

Address: Piazza del Duomo, 50122 Firenze FI, Italy

The Church of Santa Maria del Fiore is known for its impressive facade and historical significance. [33]

TRANSPORT

When it comes to traveling from Florence to Centro Storico, the journey is not only convenient, but it also offers a variety of transportation options to suit different preferences. Here are three ways to navigate the historic heart of the city.

BUS

If you're seeking an affordable and efficient means of transportation, taking the bus is the optimal choice. With a quick eight-minute journey, you can seamlessly transition from Florence to Centro Storico. Bus tickets are reasonably priced, typically ranging from €1 to €2.

TAXI

If time is of the essence and you prefer a direct and swift journey, a taxi ride stands out as the fastest option. In just five minutes, you'll get to your destination. Taxi fares may range between €7 and €10.

WALK

If you like the idea of a leisurely stroll through Florence's charming streets, you can simply walk to your destination. You'll cover the distance in approximately 17 minutes and also be able to soak in the ambiance of both the modern city and the historic center.

Although the tram lines do go through the district, stations are around the Santa Maria Novella train station, so buses or walking are a great way to get around this quarter.

EXPERIENCES

F-LIGHT FESTIVAL

Experience Centro Storico in a different light during the F-Light Festival, typically held in December. The festival transforms the city with captivating light installations, projections, and artistic displays, turning historic buildings into breathtaking works of art. The event is free, allowing visitors to wander through the illuminated streets and squares, capturing the magic of Florence after dark.

HISTORICAL INSIGHTS AT THE CHURCH OF SANTA MARIA DEL FIORE

Delve into the historical and architectural significance of the Church of Santa Maria del Fiore. Join guided tours that provide insights into the art, culture, and religious heritage embedded in this iconic landmark. Explore the stunning facade and interior, unraveling the stories behind its construction.

ESTATE FIESOLANA: SUMMER ARTS FESTIVAL

Estate Fiesolana, Florence's renowned summer arts festival, spills into Centro Storico with a plethora of cultural events. From June to September, the district hosts open-air concerts, theater performances, and art exhibitions. The diverse program caters to all artistic tastes, and many events are free or reasonably priced, providing accessible cultural experiences against the backdrop of historic Florence.

FLORENCE GELATO FESTIVAL

Indulge your sweet tooth in the heart of Centro Storico during the Florence Gelato Festival, an annual event held in April. Gelato artisans from around the world converge to showcase their delectable creations. You can purchase a Gelato Card, allowing you to sample a variety of flavors and vote for your favorite. It's a delightful and delicious way to explore Florence's historic streets.

FESTA DELLA RIFICOLONA: LANTERN FESTIVAL

Celebrate the Festa della Rificolona, a traditional lantern festival held on September 7th. Originating from rural traditions, this event sees the streets of Centro Storico illuminated with colorful paper lanterns. The festivities include a lively parade, live music, and a vibrant atmosphere. Participation is free, making it an accessible and authentic cultural experience for locals and visitors alike.

MAGGIO MUSICALE FIORENTINO: MUSICAL EXTRAVAGANZA

Centro Storico becomes a stage for the Maggio Musicale Fiorentino, an annual music festival that typically runs from late April to early July. The festival features opera, classical music concerts, and dance performances at various historic venues, including the Teatro Comunale. Ticket prices vary depending on the event.

FLORENCE TATTOO CONVENTION

If you're interested in body art, the Florence Tattoo Convention is a must-attend event. Held annually, usually in November, this convention gathers tattoo artists from around the world. Visitors can witness live tattooing, participate in workshops, and even get inked themselves.

CULTURAL PERFORMANCES AT TEATRO PUCCINI

Immerse yourself in the vibrant arts scene by attending cultural performances at Teatro Puccini. Check the schedule for plays, concerts, and other artistic events, offering an enriching experience within the historic walls of this renowned theater.

WHERE TO EAT

Here are some exceptional dining establishments that showcase the diverse and delectable flavors of the district.

TERRAZZE MICHELANGELO

This charming restaurant captures the essence of Tuscan cuisine with its emphasis on fresh, locally sourced ingredients. The menu features dishes including pizza, pasta, and their own specials. This restaurant offers a view of the city, as it is located on a terrace.

Address: Viale Michelangelo, 61, 50125 Firenze FI, Italy

BEPPA FIORAIA

A local, cozy restaurant offering traditional Tuscan cuisine with various seating areas and a view. Beppa Fioraia emphasizes the use of fresh ingredients and offers dishes including seafood, meat, pasta, pizza, and much more.

Address: Via dell'Erta Canina, 6/R, 50125 Firenze FI, Italy

PARC BISTRO

Enjoy a delightful dining experience at Parc Bistro, located near the park. Indulge in authentic Tuscan dishes prepared with locally sourced ingredients. The restaurant's terrace offers a charming setting, allowing you to savor your meal while overlooking the greenery of Parco delle Cascine.

Address: Piazzale delle Cascine, 50144 Firenze FI, Italy

YELLOW BAR

Yellow Bar is a casual yet vibrant spot known for its delicious pizzas and laid-back atmosphere. Whether you're looking for a quick bite or a leisurely meal, this pizzeria offers a menu that caters to a variety of tastes.

Address: Via del Proconsolo, 39r, 50122 Firenze FI, Italy

TRATTORIA DELL'OCA

Experience the culinary fusion of Italian and Mediterranean flavors at Trattoria dell'Oca. Located in close proximity to Teatro Puccini, this restaurant offers a sophisticated dining experience with a diverse menu, which includes meat, pasta, and desserts, that caters to a range of palates.

Address: Via Francesco Baracca, 18 r, 50127 Firenze FI, Italy

CACIO VINO TRALLALLA

Cacio Vino Trallalla is a cozy wine bar where you can enjoy a selection of Tuscan wines paired with artisanal cheeses and cured meats. The intimate setting makes it an ideal place for a relaxed evening with friends or a romantic date.

Address: Borgo Santi Apostoli, 29/R, 50123 Firenze FI, Italy

NOTE DI VINO

Unwind in the evening at Note di Vino, a charming wine bar with a selection of Tuscan wines. Paired with a variety of local cheeses and antipasti, this spot provides a relaxed atmosphere, making it an ideal place to conclude your day of exploration.

Address: Borgo dei Greci, 4, 50100 Firenze FI, Italy

IL LATINI

Located in the heart of Centro Storico, Il Latini is a culinary institution revered for its traditional Tuscan fare. Renowned for its succulent Bistecca alla Fiorentina, a mouthwatering T-bone steak, Il Latini takes pride in showcasing the bold flavors of Tuscan cuisine. The Ribollita, a hearty vegetable and bread soup, and the Pappa al Pomodoro, a tomato and bread soup, are also local favorites. The communal tables foster a convivial atmosphere, creating an authentic dining experience that reflects the warmth of Italian hospitality.

Address: Via dei Palchetti, 6R, 50123 Firenze FI, Italy

TRATTORIA CAMMILLO

For a taste of timeless elegance, Trattoria Cammillo has been enchanting patrons since 1945. Set in a historic building, this trattoria exudes classic Florentine charm. Diners rave about the Gnocchi with Gorgonzola, a delicate pasta dish that perfectly balances richness and flavor. The Osso Buco, a Milanese specialty featuring slow-cooked veal shanks, is a highlight for those seeking a hearty main course. Conclude your meal with their divine Tiramisu, a decadent treat that embodies the essence of Italian indulgence.

Address: Borgo S. Jacopo, 57/r, 50125 Firenze FI, Italy

ALL'ANTICO VINAIO

All'Antico Vinaio, a humble panini shop tucked away in a narrow alley, has become a must-visit for food enthusiasts. Famed for their generously stuffed traditional Tuscan panini, the flavors are nothing short of exceptional. Locals and tourists alike queue up for these artisanal sandwiches filled with a variety of cured meats, cheeses, and delectable spreads. The casual and lively atmosphere adds to the experience, making it the perfect spot for a quick yet unforgettable meal.

Address: Via dei Neri, 65r, 50122 Firenze FI, Italy

OSTERIA SANTO SPIRITO

Situated in the charming Piazza Santo Spirito, this osteria embodies the essence of local elegance. Osteria Santo Spirito delights patrons with dishes like Risotto al Nero di Seppia, a black squid ink risotto that tantalizes the taste buds. The Tagliata di Manzo, thinly sliced beef tenderloin, showcases the restaurant's commitment to quality ingredients. To conclude, the Tiramisu offers a sweet conclusion to your meal. The cozy ambiance and attentive service make it a favorite among those seeking an authentic Florentine dining experience.

Address: Piazza Santo Spirito, 16/R, 50125 Firenze FI, Italy

LA GIOSTRA

For a romantic dining experience, La Giostra, located near the Uffizi Gallery, is an enchanting choice. The Tortelloni Ricotta e Spinaci, a delicate pasta filled with ricotta and spinach, is a highlight for those appreciating the artistry of Italian cuisine. The Peposo, a rich and flavorful Tuscan beef stew, exemplifies the restaurant's commitment to time-honored recipes. Conclude your evening with their indulgent Chocolate Fondant, served with a scoop of vanilla gelato, in a setting that exudes intimacy and charm.

Address: Borgo Pinti, 12 R, 50121 Firenze FI, Italy

ANTICA TRATTORIA DA TITO

Antica Trattoria da Tito is a charming Tuscan trattoria known for its authentic dishes and warm atmosphere. With a menu featuring local specialties and seasonal ingredients, this restaurant provides a true taste of Tuscan culinary traditions.

Address: Via S. Gallo, 112/R, 50129 Firenze FI, Italy

OSTERIA DEL CINGHIALE BIANCO

Located in the heart of Gavinana-Galluzzo, this osteria is celebrated for its Tuscan cuisine, focusing on wild boar dishes (cinghiale). The rustic ambiance and extensive wine list complement the hearty flavors of the region.

Address: Borgo S. Jacopo, 43, 50125 Firenze FI, Italy

SHOPPING GUIDE

MERCATO CENTRALE

You cannot say you have visited Florence without having lost yourself in the Mercato Centrale. Constructed when Florence was the capital of Italy and built to a design by Giuseppe Mengoni, the large structure house and food market on the ground floor and a food court on the first floor. There are also stalls that sell souvenirs and leather goods. This market is rich in both history and significance, and it is not an experience you want to miss out on!

Address: 50123 Florence, Metropolitan City of Florence, Italy

VINTAGE FINDS AT MERCATINO DELLE PULCI

Mercatino delle Pulci, or the Flea Market, is a treasure trove of vintage finds and unique items. From antique furniture to quirky collectibles, this market is perfect for those who enjoy browsing through eclectic and one-of-a-kind pieces.

Did You Know?

Did you know that Mercato delle Pulci is not just a place to find vintage items, but it also hosts exhibitions showcasing the work of local artists and designers? Keep an eye out for these events to discover the dynamic and creative side of Florence's shopping scene.

I MOSAICI DI LASTRUCCI

This artistic workshop showcases the traditional craft of handmade terracotta. Explore a range of beautifully crafted terracotta items, including decorative pieces, pottery, and tiles, all reflecting the rich artistic heritage of the region.

Address: Via dei Macci, 9, 50122 Firenze FI, Italy

ENTERTAINMENT

TEATRO PUCCINI PERFORMANCES

Experience the cultural richness at Teatro Puccini. Attend a variety of performances, including plays, concerts, and cultural events. The intimate setting of the theater provides a unique and engaging entertainment experience, showcasing the artistic vibrancy of the district.

Address: Via delle Cascine, 41, 50144 Firenze FI, Italy

PARCO DELLE CASCINE EVENTS

Check for events and festivals hosted in Parco delle Cascine. The park occasionally becomes a venue for concerts, outdoor film screenings, and cultural gatherings. Bring a blanket, sit back, and enjoy entertainment under the open sky amid the natural beauty of the park.

Parco delle Cascine also offers a plethora of outdoor activities. Join a yoga class, participate in group workouts, or simply enjoy a jog or bike ride along the park's trails. The park becomes a lively space where residents and visitors engage in various recreational pursuits.

Address: Piazzale delle Cascine, 50144 Firenze FI, Italy

MUSIC AND MORE AT LE MURATE

Le Murate is a cultural space that hosts a variety of events, including live music performances, art exhibitions, and film screenings. Once a prison, this historic venue provides an intimate setting for those seeking diverse and eclectic entertainment options.

Address: Piazza delle Murate, 50122 Firenze FI, Italy

MAGGIO MUSICALE FIORENTINO THEATRE

Enjoy an evening in the Maggio Musicale Fiorentino Theatre, where you can attend charming classical concerts and magnificent operas – or even enjoy a show with your kids.

Address: Piazza Vittorio Gui, 1, 50144 Firenze FI, Italy

OUTDOOR ACTIVITIES IN PARCO DELLE CASCINE

While primarily a natural park, Parco delle Cascine occasionally transforms into an entertainment hub. Look out for outdoor events, concerts, and cultural festivals that take advantage of the park's spacious settings.

Address: Piazzale delle Cascine, 50144 Firenze FI, Italy

NICHE PERFORMANCES AT TEATRO DEL SALE

Teatro del Sale is a unique dining and entertainment concept, offering a combination of theatrical performances and culinary experiences. Check the schedule for themed dinners and performances, providing an immersive and memorable evening.

Address: Via dei Macci, 111/r, 50122 Firenze FI, Italy

ACCOMMODATIONS

AC HOTEL FIRENZE

AC Hotel Firenze offers a comfortable stay near Parco delle Cascine. With a range of room options, this hotel provides a convenient base for exploring the district. Enjoy modern amenities and easy access to the park, making it an ideal choice for nature lovers and those seeking tranquility.

Address: Via Luciano Bausi, 5, 50144 Firenze FI, Italy

FUORDARNO BED AND BREAKFAST

Located a few minutes away from Villa Bardini, FuordArno Bed and Breakfast offers a comfortable stay near the historical areas in Gavinana-Galluzzo. This Bed and Breakfast offers large rooms equipped with everything you might need and is only a short distance away from the main attractions you may want to visit.

Address: Lungarno Torrigiani, 3, 50125 Firenze FI, Italy

PALAZZO SAN NICCOLO

Pallazzo San Niccolo is a short walk away from Piazzale Michelangelo. Palazzo San Niccolo offers a variety of rooms to cater to your needs, including rooms, studios, apartments, and deluxe rooms.

Address: Via di S. Niccolò, 79, 50125 Firenze FI, Italy

FIRENZE AL DUOMO LUXURY BED & BREAKFAST

This luxurious bed and breakfast, a walking distance from the Cathedral of Santa Maria del Fiore, truly is a delight. Every inch of Firenze al Duomo screams elegance, and their staff works hard to make your stay memorable.

Address: Piazza del Duomo, 2, 50122 Firenze FI, Italy

OTHER NOTABLE ACCOMMODATIONS

San Firenze Suites & Spa

Address: Piazza di S. Firenze, 3/A, 50122 Firenze FI, Italy

CASA THIELE ALLA SIGNORIA

Address: Via dei Calzaiuoli, 2, 50122 Firenze FI, Italy

PALAZZO MARTELLINI RESIDENZA D'EPOCA

Address: Via Maggio, 9, 50125 Firenze FI, Italy

Centro Storico, Florence's historic hub, is a rich blend of art, history, and culinary wonders that define this enchanting district. From the breathtaking Duomo to the lively events that animate its streets, each step unravels a unique facet of this timeless neighborhood. Whether you're indulging in thematic events, savoring Tuscan specialties in cozy trattorias, or exploring the historic corridors of the Vasari Corridor, Centro Storico invites you to be a part of Florence's ongoing story. In Centro Storico, Florence extends a welcome and an invitation to actively engage with its living history.

CHAPTER 7
GAVINANA-GALLUZZO

Gavinana-Galluzzo is a fascinating chapter in the rich tapestry of history, woven with the threads of culture, conflict, and evolution. This region, situated in the south of Florence, holds stories that span centuries, offering a glimpse into the dynamic interplay of diverse influences that have shaped its identity. From its ancient roots to modern times, Gavinana-Galluzzo stands as a testament to the resilience and adaptability of a community deeply connected to its heritage.

Gavinana-Galluzzo. [34]

BRIEF HISTORICAL BACKGROUND

The history of Gavinana-Galluzzo is deeply rooted in the broader historical context of Italy, a land that has witnessed the rise and fall of empires, the flourishing of art and culture, and the struggles for independence and unity. The region's origins can be traced back to ancient times when it played a role in the Etruscan and Roman civilizations.

During the medieval period, Gavinana-Galluzzo became part of the intricate network of city-states that characterized Italy, each with its own unique character and political structure. These city-states often found themselves entangled in conflicts, alliances, and power struggles, shaping the destiny of the region.

In more recent centuries, Gavinana-Galluzzo has been witness to the transformative events of the Renaissance, witnessing the flourishing of art, literature, and scientific thought. The echoes of this cultural renaissance resonate in the architectural wonders and artistic treasures that dot the landscape.

However, Gavinana-Galluzzo, like much of Italy, did not escape the challenges of the modern era, experiencing the impact of wars, political upheavals, and societal transformations. However, the resilience of its people and the preservation of its cultural heritage have allowed Gavinana-Galluzzo to navigate the currents of time and emerge as a unique blend of tradition and modernity.

Exploring the history of Gavinana-Galluzzo invites us to delve into the layers of the past, uncovering stories of triumphs and tribulations that have shaped the character of this remarkable region. It is a journey that spans epochs, offering a glimpse into the enduring spirit of a community tethered to its roots while embracing the ever-changing tides of history.

MAIN ATTRACTIONS

CERTOSA DI FIRENZE (FLORENCE CHARTERHOUSE)

Nestled amid the rolling hills, the Certosa di Firenze, also known as Certosa di Galluzzo, is a Carthusian monastery founded in 1341. The complex includes a church, chapels, and the Grande Chiostro, a grand cloister with a fountain at its center. The peacefulness of the monastery and the surrounding gardens provide a serene escape from the bustling city life.

As of the writing of this book, operating hours are 10am to 12:30pm and then 3pm to 5:30pm every day except Monday when it is closed. Always double-check the operating hours before visiting the site.

Address: Via della Certosa, 1, 50124 Firenze FI, Italy

Nestled amid the rolling hills, the Certosa di Galluzzo is a Carthusian monastery founded in 1341. [35]

MUSEO STEFANO BARDINI

St. Michael Archangel. [36]

Museo Stefano Bardini is a museum located in a fine building that was refurbished by Stefano Bardini towards the end of the 18th century. Bardini was a well-renowned art dealer who collected high-quality objects from different periods of time. The museum has two floors, with an exquisite collection of paintings, sculptures, ceramic and furniture pieces, and fragments of the old center of Florence before its destruction. One of the most outstanding paintings in the collection is "St. Michael Archangel," painted by Antonio Del Pollaiolo.

As of the writing of this book, normal operating hours are 2pm to 7pm, Fridays to Mondays. Always double-check all operating hours before visiting the site.

Address: Via dei Renai, 37, 50125 Firenze FI, Italy

FLORENCE OBSERVATORY

For a unique experience, visit the Florence Observatory. Located nearby, it offers a chance for stargazing and panoramic views of the city. Explore the wonders of the night sky and enjoy the serene surroundings atop this vantage point.

As of the writing of this book, normal operating hours are 9am to 6pm, Mondays to Fridays, closed on Saturdays and Sundays. Always double-check times before visiting the site.

Address: Largo Enrico Fermi, 5, 50125 Firenze FI, Italy

For a unique experience, visit the Florence Observatory. [37]

Did You Know?

Did you know that Carthusian monks performed research and experimentation in Charterhouse of Galluzzo?

The Carthusian monks did a lot of scientific experimentation and research in the Charterhouse, remnants of which remain in a double vertical cornerstone clock and a sundial with a camera obscura. This historical connection adds a layer of intrigue to the Charterhouse, making it not only a religious site but also a place linked to scientific discovery.

TRANSPORT

Gavinana-Galluzzo is well-connected by various modes of transportation, allowing visitors easy access to the district and its attractions.

BUS SERVICES

The local bus network efficiently connects Gavinana-Galluzzo with the broader region, including Florence's city center. Buses provide a convenient and cost-effective means of transportation, allowing visitors to easily explore the district and its surroundings.

TAXI SERVICES

Taxis are readily available and offer a comfortable and direct mode of transportation. They are convenient for those who prefer a more personalized and flexible travel experience. Taxis can be found either at designated stands or they can be hailed on the streets.

CAR RENTALS

Car rentals are available in and around Gavinana-Galluzzo for those seeking independence in their travels. Renting a car provides the freedom to explore the picturesque Tuscan countryside and nearby attractions at one's own pace. It is advisable to familiarize yourself with local traffic regulations and parking options.

CYCLING

Gavinana-Galluzzo's scenic landscapes and relatively compact size make cycling an enjoyable and eco-friendly option. Many areas offer bike rentals, allowing visitors to pedal through vineyards, olive groves, and charming streets, providing a unique perspective of the district.

WALKING

The district's historical and cultural sites are often best explored on foot. Walking through the narrow streets of Gavinana-Galluzzo allows visitors to appreciate the local architecture, discover hidden gems, and immerse themselves in the authentic atmosphere of the area.

Did You Know?

Did you know that the district has a rich network of walking trails?

Gavinana-Galluzzo is not only accessible by traditional transportation but also boasts a network of walking trails that wind through its picturesque landscapes. These trails offer a unique opportunity for visitors to connect with nature, discover hidden gems, and enjoy breathtaking views of the surrounding hills. Whether a leisurely stroll or a more challenging hike, exploring Gavinana-Galluzzo on foot allows for a deeper appreciation of its natural beauty and cultural heritage.

EXPERIENCES

Gavinana-Galluzzo offers a variety of enriching experiences for visitors, blending cultural immersion with the region's natural beauty. Below are some thematic sightseeing, events, and tours that enhance your visit.

STARGAZING AT FLORENCE OBSERVATORY

For a celestial experience, plan an evening at the Florence Observatory. Check for scheduled stargazing sessions or themed astronomical events. This unique opportunity allows you to explore the night sky, learn about celestial bodies, and enjoy a panoramic view of Florence.

ART AND CULTURE TOUR

Explore the rich artistic heritage of Gavinana-Galluzzo by embarking on a curated art and culture tour. Visit the Basilica di San Miniato al Monte to marvel at its Romanesque architecture and exquisite artworks. The Museo di San Salvi provides insight into the district's religious and artistic history.

HISTORICAL WALKING TOURS

Join a guided walking tour through the charming streets of Gavinana-Galluzzo to discover hidden historical gems and hear captivating stories about the district's past. Walk through Piazzale Michelangelo for panoramic views and gain insights into the local architecture.

CULINARY EXPLORATION

Indulge in a culinary adventure by exploring local markets and eateries. Taste traditional Tuscan dishes and learn about the region's gastronomic delights. Consider taking a cooking class to master the art of preparing authentic Italian cuisine.

FESTIVALS AND EVENTS

Check the local calendar for festivals and events that might coincide with your visit. Whether it's a religious celebration at the Basilica di San Miniato al Monte or a community event in the town center, participating in local festivities provides a unique cultural experience.

HIKING AND NATURE TOURS

Discover the natural beauty surrounding Gavinana-Galluzzo through hiking and nature tours. Explore the scenic trails, such as those leading to Piazzale Michelangelo, and witness breathtaking views of Florence and the Tuscan countryside.

ANCONELLA GARDEN EVENTS

Although it is not open all-year round, only mid-May to September, Anconella Garden's events are very special. From the live music they offer, jazz, blues, outdoor cinema, poetry, sportive and wellness events, as well as presentations of books and meetings, you will definitely find something of interest.

One of the bonus perks to this place is that all events are free of charge. You just go and enjoy yourself.

Did You Know?

Did you know that Gavinana-Galluzzo hosts an annual cultural festival celebrating local arts and traditions?

The district takes pride in its cultural heritage, and each year, Gavinana-Galluzzo hosts a vibrant cultural festival that showcases local arts, traditions, and performances. This event provides a unique opportunity for visitors to immerse themselves in the authentic atmosphere of the district, enjoying music, dance, and art while connecting with the local community. Check the event calendar to see if your visit coincides with this lively celebration of Gavinana-Galluzzo's cultural richness.

WHERE TO EAT

Gavinana-Galluzzo offers a delightful array of dining options, from traditional Tuscan fare to contemporary culinary experiences. Here are some recommended restaurants and eateries where you can savor the local flavors:

ANTICO RISTORANTE LA CERTOSA

Nestled near the Certosa di Galluzzo, this restaurant combines Italian hospitality with a diverse menu. From wood-fired pizzas to seafood pasta, La Certosa offers a range of options, and its outdoor seating allows diners to enjoy the picturesque surroundings.

Address: Via Cassia, 1, 50023 Impruneta FI, Italy

VIA CONCEPT STORE

Indulge in a unique experience where you can not only shop for unique trinkets and souvenirs but also enjoy a hearty and delicious dinner!

Address: Via Giampaolo Orsini, 85, 50126 Firenze FI, Italy

DAZERO FIRENZE

If you're looking for a pizza restaurant, you've come to the right place. With a wide range of items on its menu and a welcoming atmosphere, enjoying a meal at DaZero Firenze will definitely be worth it.

Address: 9rosso, Lungarno Francesco Ferrucci, 50124 Firenze FI, Italy

VECCHIA OSTERIA DAL NACCHERO

An old-fashioned touch to Tuscan food, Vecchia Osteria dal Nacchero actually aims to offer the cuisine of the past, made with simple and natural foods that always wink at tradition.

Address: P.za Gavinana, 3-4/R, 50126 Firenze FI, Italy

SHOPPING GUIDE

Gavinana-Galluzzo offers a unique shopping experience, blending traditional craftsmanship with contemporary boutiques. Here's a guide to help you discover the best shopping spots in the district:

PICCOLO MERCATO DI PIAZZA ARTUSI

Dive into the local atmosphere by visiting Piccolo Mercato, a bustling market where vendors display fresh produce, artisanal cheeses, and handmade goods. It's the perfect place to experience the vibrancy of daily life and perhaps find unique souvenirs.

Address: Via Ambrogio Traversari, 50126 Firenze FI, Italy

ARTISANAL WORKSHOPS

Gavinana-Galluzzo is known for its artisanal workshops, where skilled craftsmen create handmade items ranging from pottery to leather goods. Explore these workshops to find one-of-a-kind treasures and support local craftsmanship.

VIA SENESE

This historical street is lined with charming shops and boutiques, offering a mix of traditional and contemporary wares. Via Senese provides a diverse shopping experience – from locally crafted jewelry to stylish clothing.

BOOKWORM'S HAVEN – L'ANGOLO DEL LIBRO

L'Angolo del Libro is a haven for book lovers. Browse through a carefully curated selection of books, including works by local authors, art publications, and classic literature. The cozy ambiance and knowledgeable staff make it an inviting space for literary exploration. Look out for special events, book signings, and discussions that occasionally occur in the store.

Address: Via Filippo Webb, 1, 50126 Firenze FI, Italy

BOUTIQUE VINEYARDS

Discover boutique vineyards in the surrounding hills where you can purchase local wines directly from the producers. Many vineyards offer wine tastings, allowing you to select your favorite bottles to enjoy during your visit or take home as souvenirs.

Did You Know?

Did you know that Via Senese has been a commercial hub since medieval times?

Via Senese, with its historical charm and array of shops, has served as a commercial hub since medieval times. The street has witnessed centuries of trade and commerce, evolving to meet the changing needs of the community. Today, it continues to be a vibrant shopping destination, offering a mix of traditional and modern establishments. Exploring Via Senese provides a delightful shopping experience and connects you with the rich commercial history of Gavinana-Galluzzo.

ENTERTAINMENT

While Gavinana-Galluzzo may be more renowned for its historical and cultural attractions, there are several entertainment options that add to the overall experience of the district. Here are some recommendations for leisure and entertainment:

TEATRO REIMS

Art and theatre lovers, this is for you. Located in the east of Florence, Teatro Reims offers multiple performances of prose and music. Prose performances like *It's the Garden's Fault*, *Noises Off-Stage*, and *His Name Will Be Andrea*, and music performances like Frida Kahlo *Love and Revolution*, The Pilgrims, and Freedom – Teatro Reims has it all.

Attending a show and delving into its artistic, authentic atmosphere will guarantee an unforgettable night.

Address: Via Reims, 30, 50126 Firenze FI, Italy

PARKS AND GREEN SPACES

Enjoy leisurely strolls or picnics in the parks and green spaces throughout Gavinana-Galluzzo. These areas, such as the gardens surrounding Villa Le Piazzole, offer a tranquil retreat for relaxation and casual outdoor activities.

LOCAL PUBS AND BARS

Unwind in the evening by exploring local pubs and bars in Gavinana-Galluzzo. Some establishments may offer live music, providing a laid-back atmosphere for socializing with locals and fellow travelers.

CULTURAL EVENTS AT CERTOSA DI GALLUZZO

In addition to its historical significance, the Certosa di Galluzzo occasionally transforms its courtyard into a venue for open-air concerts, like the FilArmonia, as well as wedding receptions and private parties. This unique setting provides a captivating backdrop for musical performances, allowing visitors to enjoy live music in the atmospheric surroundings of the monastery. Keep an eye on event listings to see if any concerts coincide with your visit, offering a memorable blend of entertainment and cultural immersion.

LOCAL FESTIVALS AND CELEBRATIONS

Participate in local festivals and celebrations, often including live music, performances, and cultural events. Whether it's a religious procession or a community celebration, these events offer a chance to experience the lively spirit of Gavinana-Galluzzo.

ACCOMMODATIONS

Gavinana-Galluzzo offers a range of accommodations, from charming guesthouses to elegant villas, providing visitors with comfortable options that complement the district's rich historical and cultural ambiance. Here are some recommended places to stay:

AGRITURISMO LE MACINE

For a rustic and unique stay, consider Agriturismo Le Machine, located on the outskirts of Campo di Marte. This farmhouse accommodation allows guests to experience the tranquility of the countryside while being close to the attractions of the district.

Address: Viuzzo del Pozzetto, 1, 50126 Firenze FI, Italy

ITALIANA HOTELS FLORENCE

Enjoy a luxurious stay at Italiana Hotels Florence. This hotel is close to all the main attractions you might want to visit. Italiana Hotels Florence offers spacious rooms with free Wi-Fi, TVs, an elegant restaurant, a pool, and a gym.

Address: Viale Europa, 205, 50126 Firenze FI, Italy

VILLA MERLO BIANCO

Located just outside the city center of Florence, Villa Merlo Bianco offers a warm, homely stay in a restored guesthouse. Villa Merlo Bianco is surrounded by a large garden and each guest room has its own individual style.

Address: Via di Ripoli, 82, 50126 Firenze FI, Italy

B&B OLIVER

Located near the Certosa di Galluzzo, this historic bed and breakfast exudes charm and hospitality. B&B Oliver offers cozy rooms, a garden terrace, and a welcoming ambiance, providing a delightful base for exploring the district.

Address: Via Camillo Barni, 54, 50125 Firenze FI, Italy

BORGO BOTTAIA

Located just on the outskirts of Gavinana-Galluzzo, Borgo Bottaia provides a tranquil escape with its Tuscan-style apartments surrounded by olive groves. The accommodations are equipped with modern amenities, and the property features a pool and picturesque views.

Address: Via delle Fonti, 62Q, 50012 Bagno a Ripoli FI, Italy

Did You Know?

Did you know that some accommodations in Gavinana-Galluzzo are housed in renovated historic buildings, preserving the district's architectural heritage?

Several accommodations in Gavinana-Galluzzo are dedicated to preserving the district's architectural heritage by converting historic buildings into charming places to stay. Whether it's a renovated villa, a former monastery, or a farmhouse turned agriturismo, these accommodations allow guests to experience the unique charm of Gavinana-Galluzzo while enjoying modern comforts. Staying in such establishments provides an opportunity to be immersed in the rich history and cultural ambiance of the district.

CHAPTER

8 City Itineraries and Programs

If you're not up for the usual travel guide jargon and just want a shortcut to the best spots in Florence without the hassle of planning, you're in luck. This chapter is your go-to guide for quick and easy itineraries that'll have you navigating the city's most beautiful districts without spending too much time planning your days.

If you're in Florence for just a week, try to make every moment count. [38]

A WEEK IN FLORENCE – DISTRICT DELIGHTS

If you're in Florence for just a week and want to make every moment count, following this itinerary will be a good idea. It maps out a journey through four distinct districts – each offering a unique flavor of Florence, ensuring you experience the art, history, cuisine, and vibrant culture that make this city truly unforgettable.

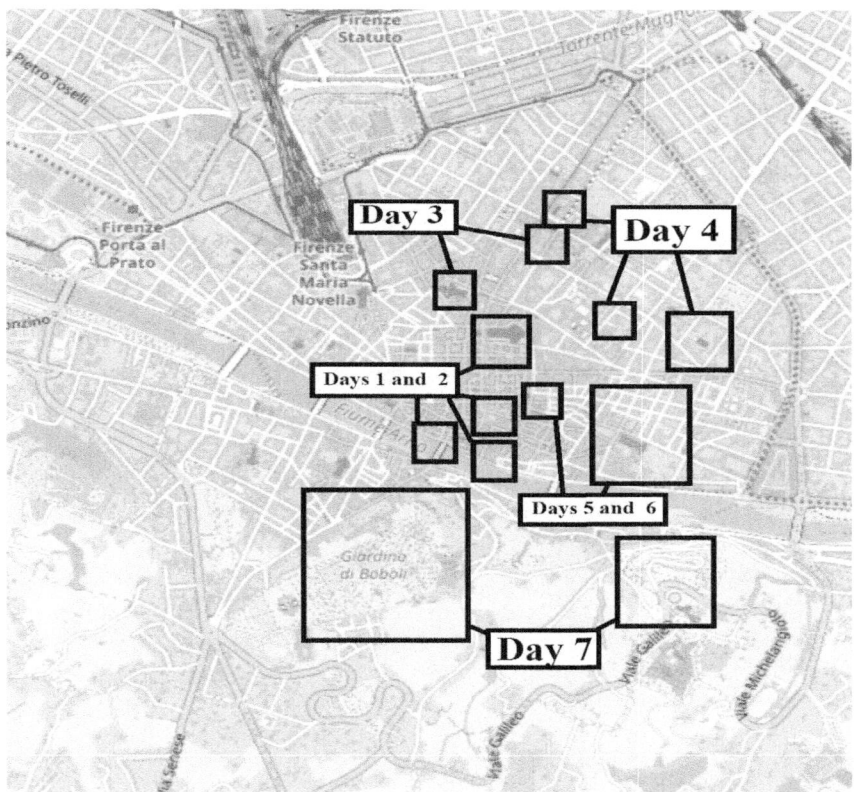

A week in Florence.[39]

DAYS 1-2: HISTORIC CENTER EXTRAVAGANZA

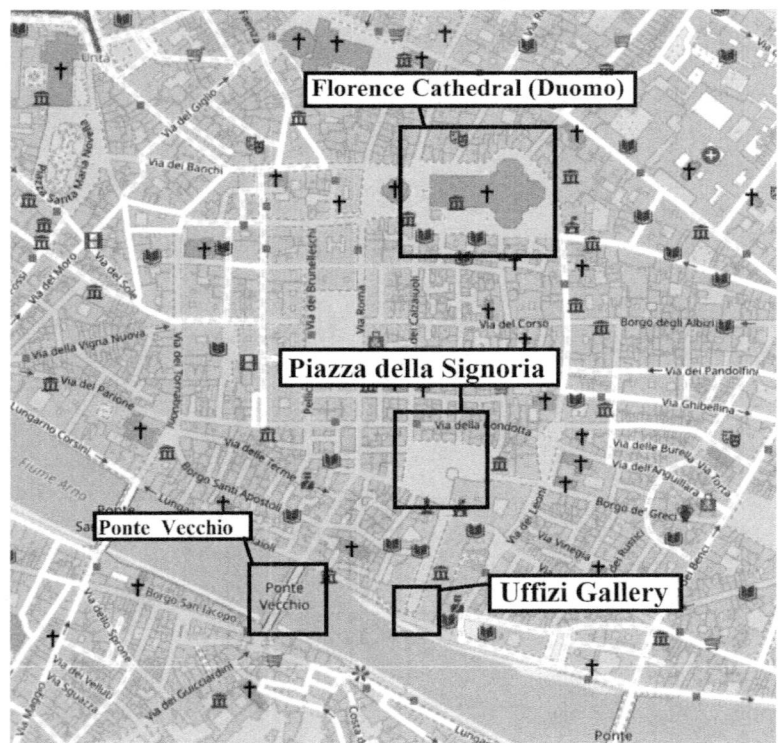

Days 1 and 2.[40]

104 | FLORENCE TRAVEL GUIDE

DAY 1:

+ **Morning:**
    - ✓ Begin your day at the Florence Cathedral (Duomo) and marvel at the intricate details of the facade.

Florence Cathedral (Duomo) QR Code

+ **Afternoon:**
    - ✓ Explore the Uffizi Gallery, home to an extensive collection of Renaissance art (pre-book tickets: €20). You can walk the short distance from the Duomo.

Uffizi Gallery QR Code

+ **Evening:**
    - ✓ Savor a traditional Tuscan dinner at Trattoria La Casalinga, located near Ponte Vecchio.

Address: Via dei Michelozzi, 9R, 50125 Firenze FI, Italy

    - ✓ Take a stroll along the Arno River, enjoying the evening ambiance.

DAY 2:

+ **Morning:**
  - ✓ Wander through Piazza della Signoria and admire famous sculptures like Michelangelo's David.

Piazza della Signoria QR Code

+ **Afternoon:**
  - ✓ Visit Ponte Vecchio and enjoy the feat of architecture.

Ponte Vecchio QR Code

A very short walk from Piazza della Signoria

✦ **Evening:**
  - ✓ *Attend a live performance at Teatro Verdi, a historic venue with a diverse cultural calendar.*

Address: Via Ghibellina, 99, 50122 Firenze FI, Italy

Teatro Verdi QR Code

Walking and public transportation take approximately the same time.

Public transportation: Walk to the Santa maria Soprano bus stop, take the C1 towards Parterre and get off at the Verdi bus stop. Then walk to the Tatro Verdi.

DAYS 3-4: SAN LORENZO SECRETS

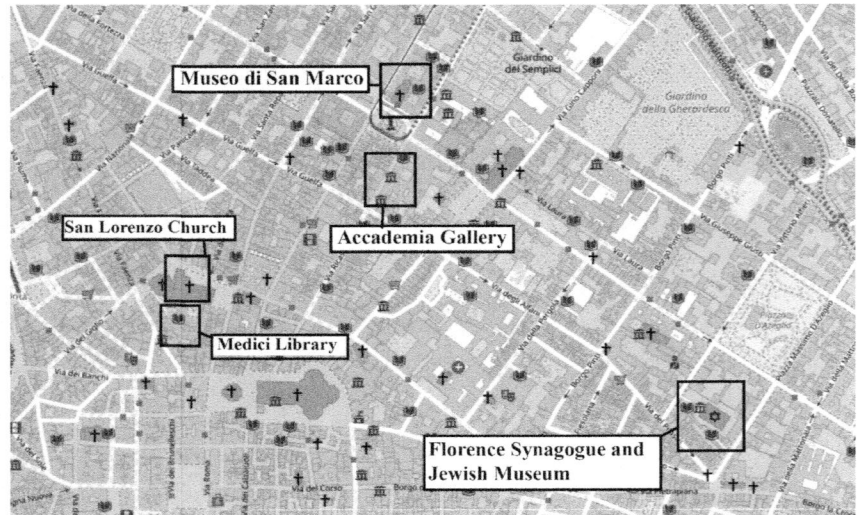

Days 3 and 4.⁴¹

DAY 3:

+ **Morning:**
  - ✓ Explore the San Lorenzo Church and its adjoining Medici Library. Discover the Medici Chapels, a must-see for art and history enthusiasts.

Medici Library Qr Code San Lorenzo Church QR Code

+ **Afternoon:**
  - ✓ Head to the Accademia Gallery to marvel at Michelangelo's David (Book tickets: €16). You can walk the almost 600 meters from San Lorenzo.

Accademia Gallery QR Code

+ **Evening:**
  - ✓ Dine at Trattoria Mario, a beloved spot offering authentic Florentine dishes.

Address: Via Rosina, 2r, 50123 Firenze FI, Italy

  - ✓ Enjoy a nightcap at Procacci, a historic wine bar in the San Lorenzo area.

Address: Via de' Tornabuoni, 64R, 50123 Firenze FI, Italy

DAY 4:

- **Morning:**
  - ✓ Take a guided tour of the Florence Synagogue and Jewish Museum to delve into the city's rich Jewish history (Tour cost: €10).

Florence Synagogue and Jewish Museum QR Code

  - ✓ Explore the nearby Museo di San Marco, which is known for its religious art.

Museo di San Marco QR Code

- **Afternoon:**
  - ✓ Lunch at Ruth's Kosher Vegetarian Restaurant for a unique culinary experience.

Address: Via Luigi Carlo Farini, 2a, 50121 Firenze FI, Italy

  - ✓ Discover the neighborhood's hidden art studios and workshops, showcasing local craftsmanship.

✦ **Evening:**
 ✓ *Attend an evening performance at Teatro della Pergola, one of the oldest theaters in Florence.*

Address: Via della Pergola, 12/32, 50121 Firenze FI, Italy

Teatro della Pergola QR Code

DAYS 5-6: SANTA CROCE VIBES

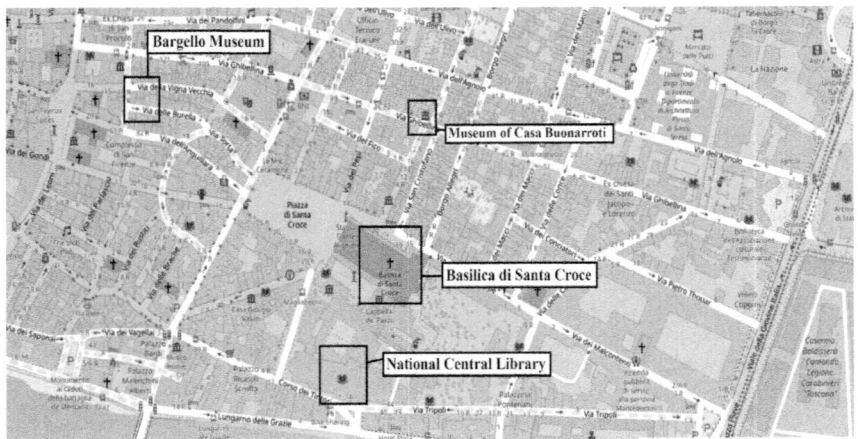

Days 5 and 6[42]

DAY 5:

+ **Morning:**
  - ✓ Visit the Bargello Museum, an often overlooked gem housing sculptures by Michelangelo and Donatello (Entrance fee: €12).

Bargello Museum QR Code

+ **Afternoon:**
  - ✓ Lunch at Casa Toscana, offering a delightful mix of traditional and innovative dishes.

Address: Via Giovanni Da Verrazzano, 3/5 r, 50122 Firenze FI, Italy

  - ✓ Visit the National Central Library, a hidden gem for book lovers. It's a short 700m walk from Bargello Museum.

National Central Library QR Code

+ **Evening:**
  - ✓ Dinner and a stroll through the city.

DAY 6:

+ **Morning:**
    ✓ Begin your day at the Basilica di Santa Croce, the final resting place of notable Italians like Michelangelo and Galileo, exploring its impressive chapels.

Basilica di Santa Croce QR Code

    ✓ Wander through the neighborhood's artisanal shops, known for unique handmade products.

+ **Afternoon:**
    ✓ Lunch at Canto del Ramerino, an elegant restaurant known for its Tuscan specialties.

Address: Via di S. Giuseppe, 38, 50122 Firenze FI, Italy

    ✓ Visit the Museum of Casa Buonarroti, housing works by Michelangelo (Entrance fee: €8). It's a short 200m walk from the basilica.

Museum of Casa Buonarroti QR Code

+ **Evening:**
    ✓ Enjoy an evening walk through the district, taking in the historic ambiance.

DAY 7: OLTRARNO UNVEILED

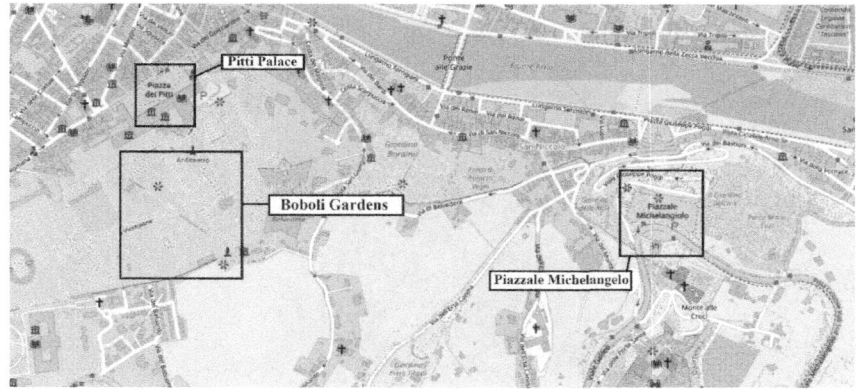

Day 7.⁴³

+ **Morning:**
    ✓ Begin your day at the *Pitti Palace*, exploring its art collections and *Boboli Gardens* (entrance fee: €16).
    ✓ Cross the *Ponte Santa Trinita* for a different perspective and capture stunning city views.

Pitti Palace QR Code   Boboli Gardens QR Code

+ **Afternoon:**
    ✓ Lunch at *Osteria Santo Spirito*, a charming eatery in the heart of Oltrarno.

Address: Piazza Santo Spirito, 16/R, 50125 Firenze FI, Italy

    ✓ Explore the neighborhood's charming streets and artisan workshops.

- **Evening:**
    - ✓ Dine at Beppa Fioraia, a popular restaurant with a diverse menu.

Address: Via dell'Erta Canina, 6/R, 50125 Firenze FI, Italy

- ✓ Conclude your week with a sunset walk up to Piazzale Michelangelo, where you can enjoy breathtaking views of Florence.

Piazzale Michelangelo QR Code

From Pitti Palace, you can take public transportation: Walk to Pitti bus stop, then take the C3 towards Piazza Beccaria and get off at Torrigiani Chiesa Luteran and then hike the 1.2km to the Piazzale.

Remember to check the attractions' opening hours, book tickets in advance, and, most importantly, savor every moment of your week-long exploration of this magnificent city.

A THREE-DAY TRIP TO ISOLOTTO-LEGNAIA AND CAMPO DI MARTE

If you're looking for a getaway that blends local charm, cultural immersion, and a touch of sports and leisure, the Isolotto-Legnaia and Campo di Marte districts are your hidden gems. This tailored three-day itinerary invites you to explore a side of Florence often overlooked by the crowds.

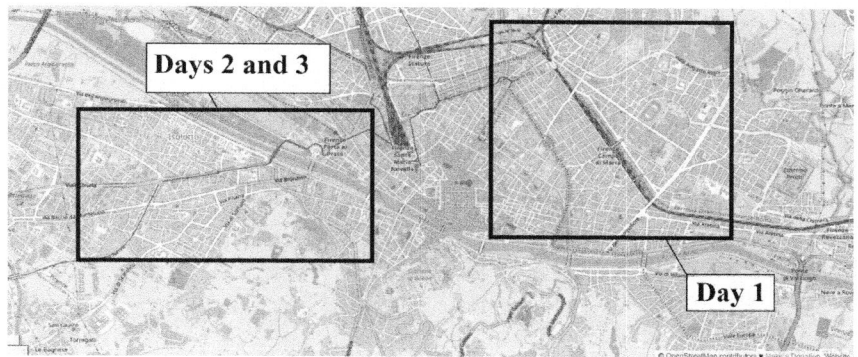

3 days in Isolotto-Legnaia and Campo di Marte.[44]

DAY 1: CAMPO DI MARTE

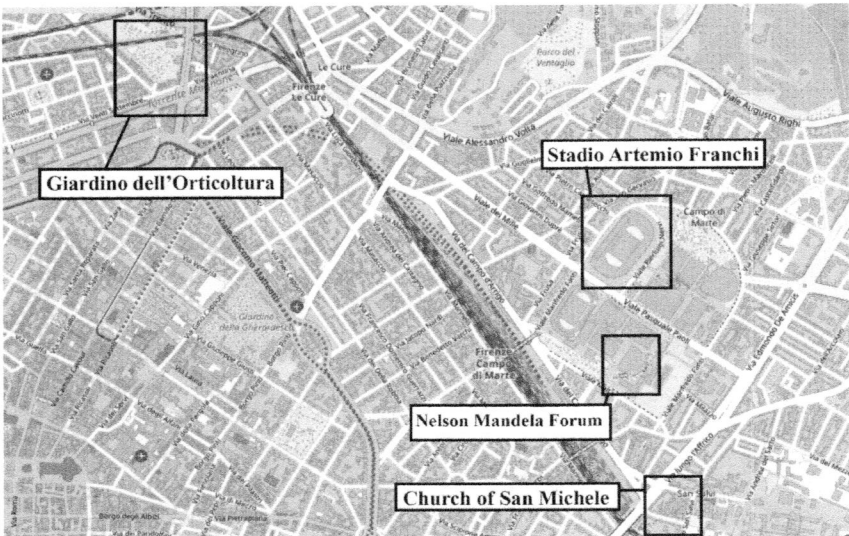

Day 1 in Campo di Marte.[45]

+ **Morning:**
    ✓ Breakfast and stroll through the Giardino dell'Orticoltura, a tranquil botanical garden perfect for a serene morning.

+ **Afternoon:**
    ✓ Lunch at Al-Turk Kebab and Pizzeria

Address: Viale dei Mille, 8/r, 50131 Firenze FI, Italy

   ✓ Visit to the iconic Stadio Artemio Franchi, the home of the Fiorentina football club. Take a guided tour to explore its history and significance.

   ✓ Explore the Nelson Mandela Forum, a hub for events and concerts, and check for ongoing events during your visit.

You can walk th 2.3 km or take public transportation.

Public Transportation: Walk to L. Il Magnifico Liberta' station and take the 20 bus to Campo d'Arrigo Sette Senti, then walk about 850m to the stadium. The Nelson Mandela Forum is right next to it.

Stadio Artemio Franchi QR Code   Nelson Mandela Forum QR Code

+ **Evening:**

   ✓ *Dine at Il Pallaio for a delightful fusion of Tuscan and Mediterranean cuisine.*

Address: Via Damiano Chiesa, 1 rosso, 50137 Firenze FI, Italy

   ✓ *Visit the Church of San Michele in San Salvi.*

You can walk the 1.6km or take public transportation.

Public transportation: Walk to Campo d'Arrigo Sette Senti bus stop, take the 20 bus to Lungo L'Affrico, then walk about 250m to the church.

Church of San Michele in San Salvi QR Code

DAY 2: ISOLOTTO-LEGNAIA

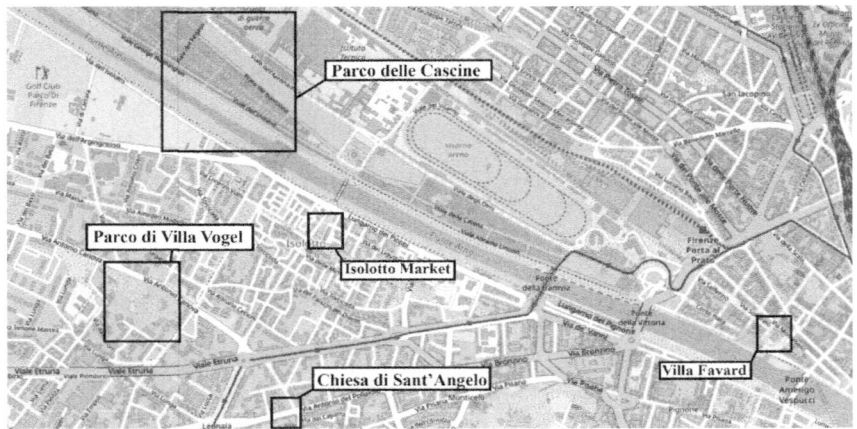

Days 2 amd 3 in Isolotto[46]

+ **Morning:**

Start your day with a visit to Parco di Villa Vogel, a peaceful park with lush greenery.

Parco di Villa Vogel QR Code

+ **Afternoon:**

Lunch and visit the Chiesa di Sant'Angelo a Legnaia, a charming church with historical significance.

You can walk the 1.2km or take public transportation.

Public transportation: Take the 77 bus from Canova Villa Vogel to Foggini Baccio Da Montelupo, then walk to the church.

Chiesa di Sant'Angelo a Legnaia QR Code

+ **Evening:**

Dinner and relax in Parco delle Cascine, the largest public park in Florence, and stroll along the Arno River.

Walking and public transport take almost the same time.

Public transportation: Take the T1.3 bus from Talenti bus stop to Cascine, then walk to the T1 Cascine – Carlo Monni bus stop and take the 55 bus to Ippodromo Del Visarno. From there, it's a 2 minute walk to the park.

Parco delle Cascine QR Code

DAY 3: **ISOLOTTO-LEGNAIA**

✦ **Morning:**
  ✓ Visit the Isolotto Market and explore the Isolotto neighborhood, known for its charming architecture and local shops.

Isolotto Market QR Code

✦ **Afternoon:**
  ✓ Visit the historic Villa Favard, known for its beautiful gardens and architecture.

You can walk the 2.3km or take public transportation.

Public transportation: Walk about 800m to the Talenti bus stop and take the T1.3 bus to Porta Al Prato-Leopolda. Then walk 600m to the villa.

Villa Favard QR Code

✦ **Evening:**
  ✓ Dinner and conclude your trip with a leisurely evening walk through the Isolotto-Legnaia district, taking in the local ambiance.

A THREE-DAY TRIP TO RIFREDI

In a city as rich and diverse as Florence, the less-explored neighborhoods often hold hidden gems waiting to be uncovered. Imagine strolling through historic gardens, immersing yourself in local culture, and savoring Tuscan delights in family-run trattorias. This itinerary has it all!

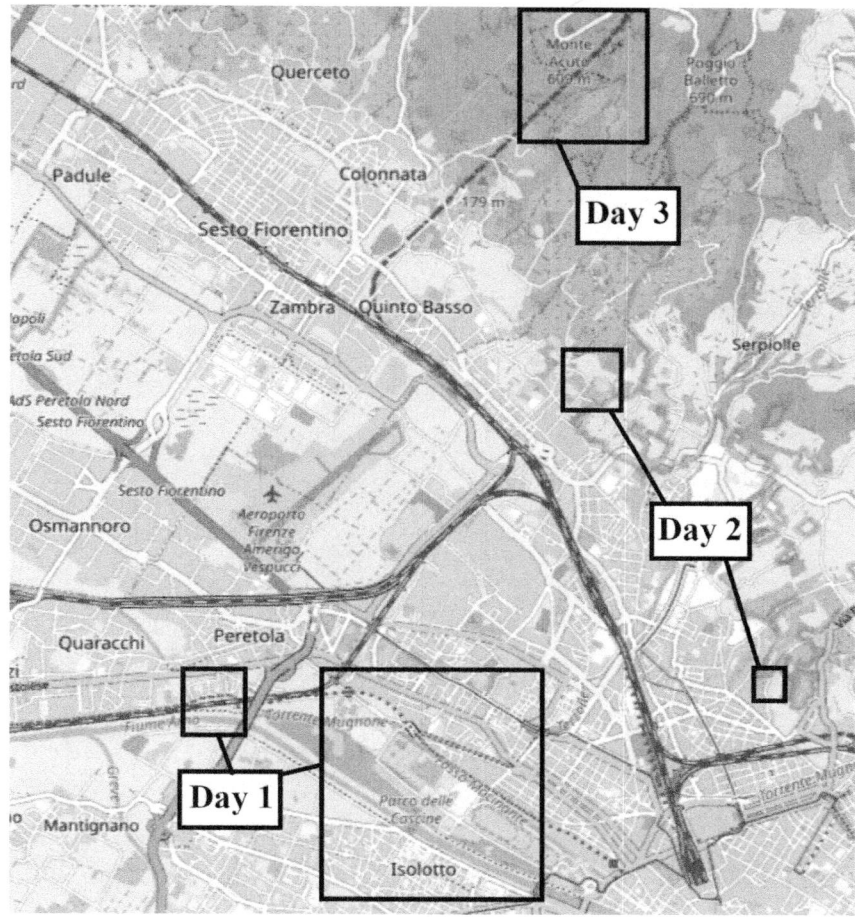

3 days in Rifredi.[47]

DAY 1

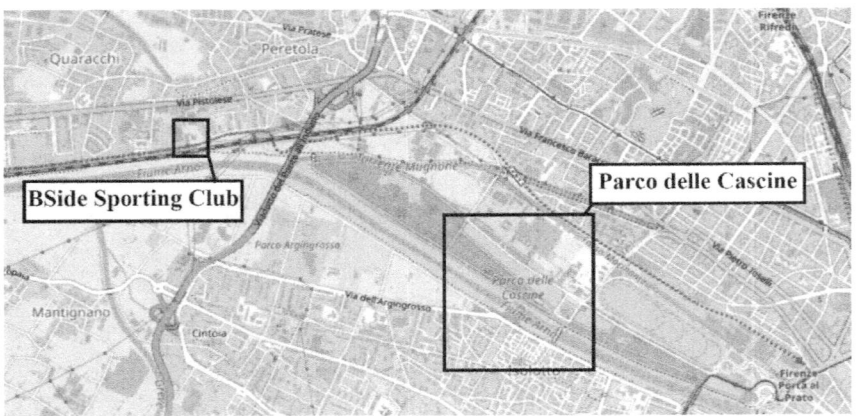

Day 1 in Rifredi.[48]

+ **Morning:**

    ✓ Start your day with a leisurely breakfast at Chiosco Le Mulina, a café inside Parco delle Cascine.

Address: Viale dell'Aeronautica, 50144 Firenze FI, Italy

    ✓ Explore the Parco delle Cascine, taking in the greenery and enjoying a morning walk.

Parco delle Cascine QR Code

+ **Afternoon:**
  - ✓ Lunch at Other Side with its beautiful atmosphere and garden.

Address: Via Pistoiese, 205, 50145 Firenze FI, Italy

  - ✓ Relax at the BSide Firenze Nord, perhaps enjoying a swim or a tennis match (40 minute walk from Parco delle Cascine).

The sporting club is close enough to walk.

BSide Sporting Club QR Code

+ **Evening:**
  - ✓ Dine at Fratelli Briganti, known for its cozy ambiance and excellent Tuscan cuisine.

Address: Piazza Giovambattista Giorgini, 12/R, 50134 Firenze FI, Italy

  - ✓ Take a stroll through the residential streets of Rifredi, experiencing the local neighborhood vibe.

DAY 2:

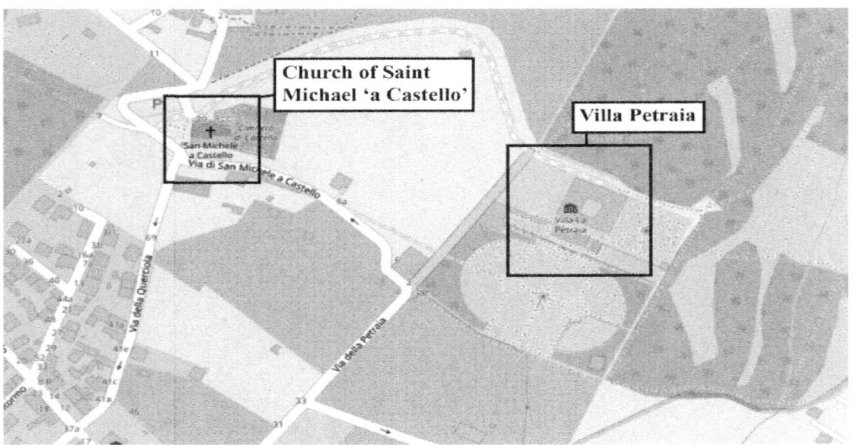

Villa Petraia and Church of Saint Michael 'a Castello'.

OpenStreetMap Contributors https://www.openstreetmap.org

✦ **Morning:**

   ✓ Visit Villa Petraia, a Medici family villa with beautiful gardens. Beside the villa, pass by the Church of Saint Michael 'a Castello' and marvel at the beauty of this Catholic church.

Villa Petraia QR Code   Church of Saint Michael 'a Castello' QR Code

✦ **Afternoon:**

  ✓ Lunch at Osteria de'Golosi, a local eatery offering traditional Tuscan dishes.

Address: Via del Ponte alle Mosse, 105 rosso, 50144 Firenze FI, Italy

  ✓ Visit Museo Stibbert, home to a unique collection of armor, costumes, and art (entrance fee: €8).

Walk about 1 km to Viale Sestese 1_V and take bus number 2 to Panciatichi Dalmazia, then bus 20 to Romito Tanucci. The museum is about a 1.4 km walk from the station.

Museo Stibbert QR Code

✦ **Evening**

  ✓ Dine at Ristorante Pizzeria Da Franco, offering a blend of traditional and innovative Tuscan dishes.

  ✓ Take a leisurely evening walk through the district, soaking in the local ambiance.

DAY 3:

MORNING AND AFTERNOON:

- ✓ Embark on a hike up to the panoramic viewpoint at Monte Morello (42 minutes from Rifredi), offering stunning views of Florence.
- ✓ Picnic lunch with a view at Monte Morello.

We would recommend taking a car to and from Monte Morello

Monte Morello QR Code

+ **Evening:**
  - ✓ Return to the city center for dinner at Pesca Palla, a cozy restaurant with a homely atmosphere.

Address: Via Carlo del Prete, 21 rosso, 50127 Firenze FI, Italy

AN ADDITIONAL DAY 4 (DEPENDING ON TRAVEL TIMES)

+ **Morning:**
  - ✓ Enjoy a leisurely breakfast at Melaleuca Firenze, a local favorite known for its creative dishes.
  - ✓ Take a final stroll through the Rifredi district, visiting any shops or spots you might have missed.

+ **Afternoon:**
  - ✓ Pack up and check out from your accommodation.
  - ✓ Depending on your departure time, grab a quick lunch at a restaurant near your accommodation before heading to the train station or airport.

A WEEKEND GETAWAY IN CENTRO STORICO

If you're short on time but eager to soak in the iconic beauty of Florence, this two-day itinerary is tailored just for you. Get ready for a whirlwind adventure through narrow cobblestone streets, past architectural wonders, and into the very soul of the city.

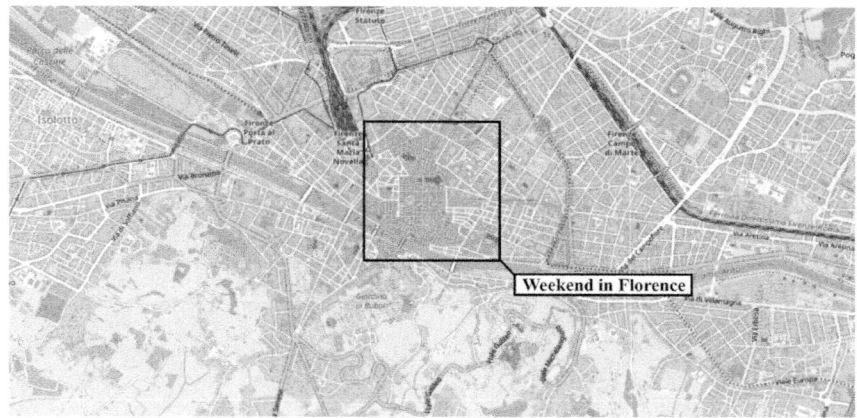

A weekend in Centro Storico.[49]

DAY 1:

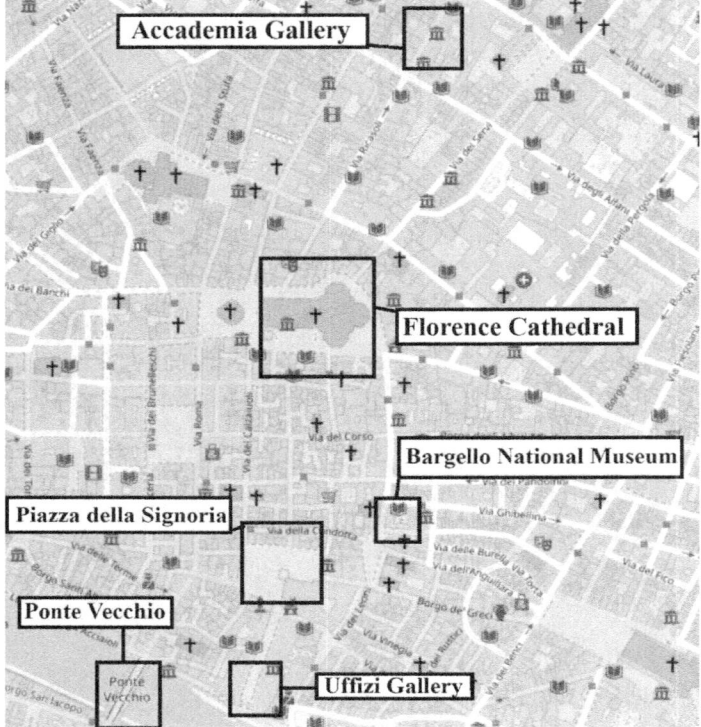

A 2-day adventure in Florence.⁵⁰

+ **Morning:**

Start your day at the iconic Florence Cathedral (Duomo). Marvel at the intricate details of the Baptistery and climb Giotto's Bell Tower for panoramic views (book tickets: €18).

Florence Cathedral (Duomo) QR Code

+ **Afternoon:**
    ✓ Lunch at All'Antico Vinaio, a renowned sandwich shop offering delicious paninis (€5 - €8).

Address: Via dei Neri, 65r, 50122 Firenze FI, Italy

    ✓ Visit the Accademia Gallery, home to Michelangelo's David (book tickets: €16).

This is a 7 minute walk.

Accademia Gallery QR Code

+ **Evening:**
    ✓ Dinner at Osteria Santo Spirito, a charming eatery in the Oltrarno district.

Address: Piazza Santo Spirito, 16/R, 50125 Firenze FI, Italy

    ✓ Take a leisurely evening stroll across Ponte Vecchio, admiring the sunset over the Arno River.

Walking and taking public transport is almost the same in time. Walking is about 1.1km

Public transportation: Walk to Cavour Palazzo Medici bus stop, take the C1 bus to Roma Duomo and walk about 500m to Ponte Vecchio.

Ponte Vecchio QR Code

DAY 2:

+ **Morning:**
    - ✓ *Begin your day at the Florence Bargello National Museum, showcasing Renaissance sculptures and decorative arts (entrance fee: €12).*

Stroll through Piazza della Signoria, admiring outdoor sculptures and the historic Palazzo Vecchio.

Bargello Museum QR Code

Piazza della Signoria QR Code

+ **Afternoon:**

Lunch at Trattoria ZaZa, a popular spot offering a variety of Tuscan dishes (€15 - €25).

Address: Piazza del Mercato Centrale, 26r, 50123 Firenze FI, Italy

- ✓ *Explore the Uffizi Gallery, home to masterpieces by Botticelli, Michelangelo, and Leonardo da Vinci (pre-book tickets: €20).*

It's about a 4-minute walk to the gallery.

Uffizi Gallery QR Code

✦ **Evening:**

Dinner at La Giostra, an elegant restaurant known for its Tuscan specialties (€30 – €50).

Address: Borgo Pinti, 12 R, 50121 Firenze FI, Italy

- ✓ Conclude your visit with a gelato from Gelateria dei Neri, a local favorite.

Address: Via dei Neri, 9/11R, 50122 Firenze FI, Italy

This two-day itinerary is designed for those with limited time, offering the perfect blend of Florence's artistic treasures, historical landmarks, and culinary delights. Ensure you book tickets in advance for popular attractions to make the most of your short stay in Centro Storico.

A FOUR-DAY TRIP AROUND FLORENCE

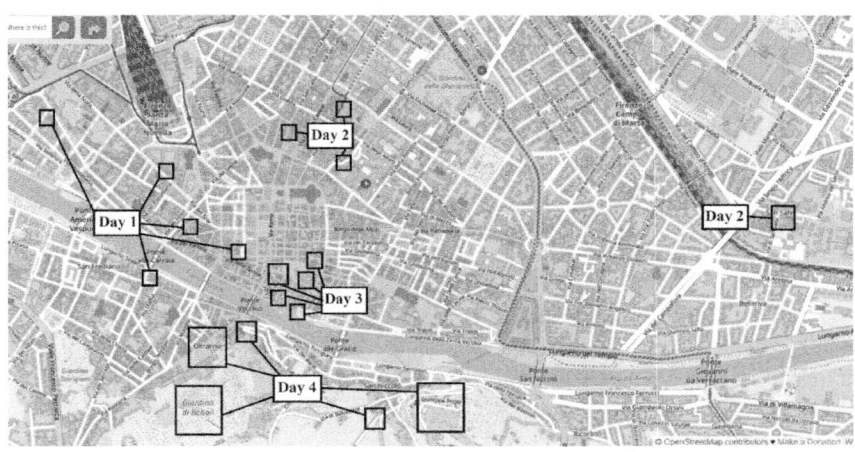

A 4-day trip around Florence.[51]

If you're seeking a one-of-a-kind adventure that goes beyond the typical tourist trail, this four-day exploration promises surprises at every turn. With its rich history and vibrant culture, Florence has more to offer than meets the eye.

DAY 1:

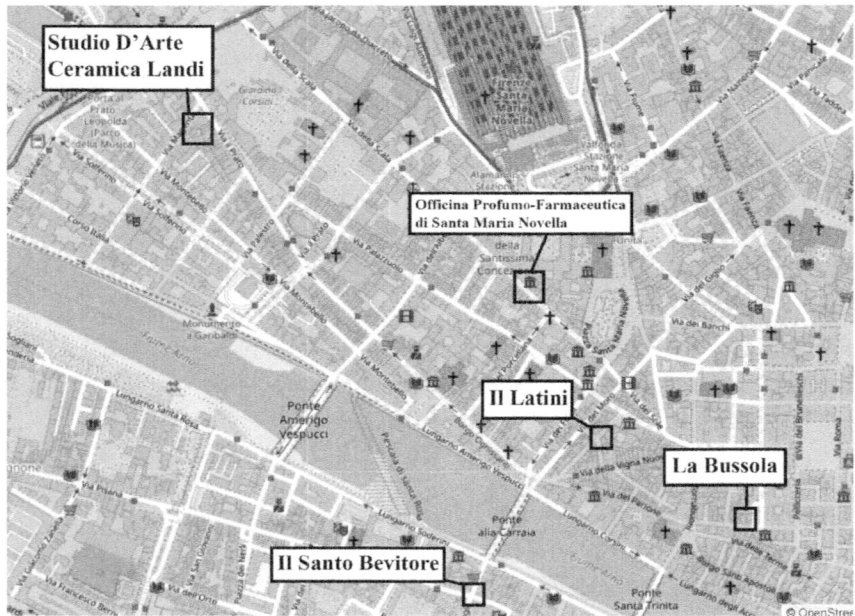

Day 1.⁵²

+ **Morning:**

    ✓ *Participate in a hands-on ceramics workshop at Studio D'Arte Ceramica Landi, a local artisan's studio (workshop cost: €80).*

Studio D'Arte Ceramica Landi QR Code

+ **Afternoon:**
- ✓ Lunch at La Bussola, a contemporary eatery offering a fusion of traditional and modern Tuscan flavors.

Address: Via Porta Rossa, 56r, 50123 Firenze FI, Italy

Or:

- ✓ Savor lunch at Il Santo Bevitore, a popular restaurant in the Oltrarno district known for its innovative dishes.

Address: Via Santo Spirito, 64r, 50125 Firenze FI, Italy

- ✓ Experience one of the world's oldest pharmacies, the Officina Profumo-Farmaceutica di Santa Maria Novella, and take part in creating unique scents. (workshop cost: €45).

Address: Via Roma, 2, 50123 Firenze FI, Italy

Officina Profumo-Farmaceutica di Santa Maria Novella QR Code

+ **Evening:**
- ✓ Dine at Il Latini, a legendary Florentine trattoria known for its hearty Tuscan fare and communal dining experience (€40 - €60).

Address: Via dei Palchetti, 6R, 50123 Firenze FI, Italy

DAY 2:

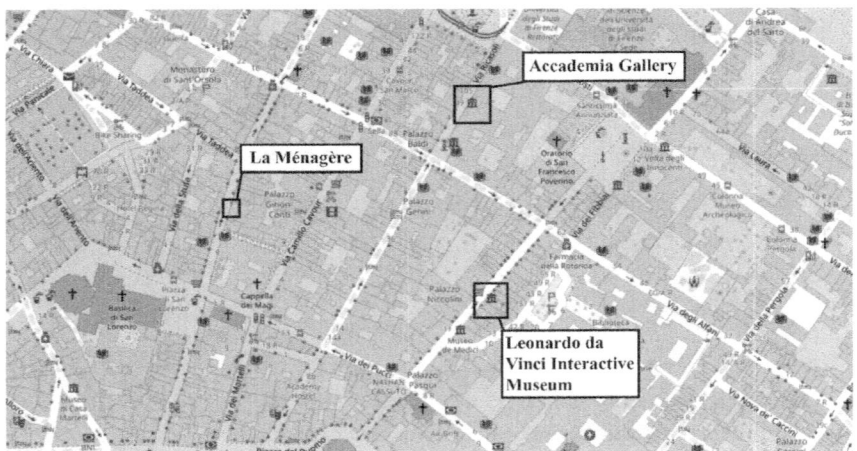

Day 2.⁵³

+ **Morning:**
  ✓ Visit the Accademia Gallery to marvel at Michelangelo's David and participate in a private sketching class led by a local artist (class cost: €25).
  ✓ Enjoy brunch at La Ménagère, a trendy concept store and café in the San Lorenzo district.

  Address: Via de' Ginori, 8/R, 50123 Firenze FI, Italy

Accademia Gallery QR Code

+ **Afternoon:**

   ✓ *Explore the Leonardo da Vinci Interactive Museum, an interactive experience showcasing the inventions of the Renaissance polymath (entrance fee: €12).*

Leonardo da Vinci Interactive Museum QR Code

+ **Evening:**

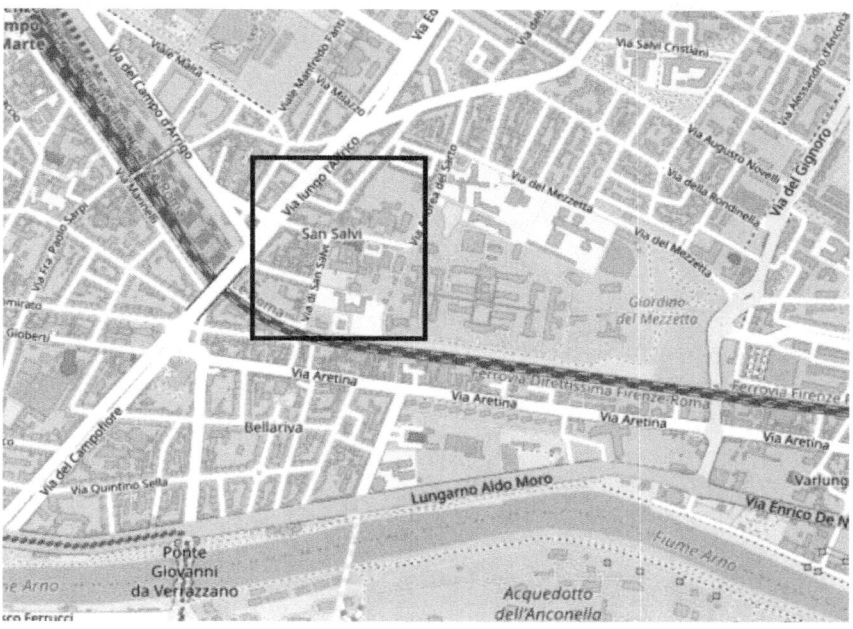

San Salvi.[54]

   ✓ *Discover the street art scene in the San Salvi neighborhood with a guided tour led by local artists (tour cost: €20).*

DAY 3:

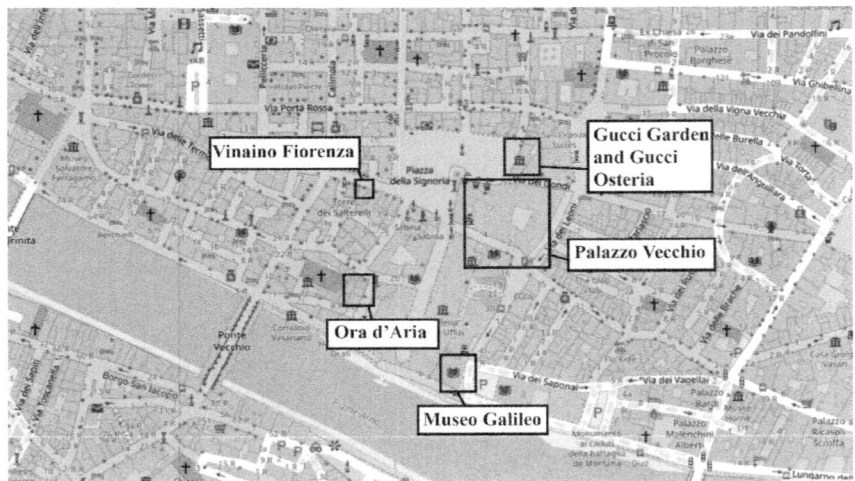

Day 3.[55]

+ **Morning:**

  ✓ Start your day at Palazzo Vecchio, but with a twist – join a private early-morning tour to explore hidden chambers and secret passages (tour cost: €30).

  ✓ For breakfast, grab a tasty sandwich from Vinaino Fiorenza.

  Address: Via Vacchereccia, 13r, 50122 Firenze FI, Italy

Palazzo Vecchio QR Code

- **Afternoon:**
  - ✓ Visit the Museo Galileo, an institution dedicated to the history of science and the Medici collections (entrance fee: €10).
  - ✓ Explore the Gucci Garden, a unique museum celebrating the iconic fashion house (entrance fee: €10).
  - ✓ Lunch at Gucci Osteria, a restaurant by Michelin-starred chef Massimo Bottura, located within the Gucci Garden.

Address: P.za della Signoria, 10, 50122 Firenze FI, Italy

Museo Galileo QR Code   Gucci Garden QR Code

- **Evening:**
  - ✓ Dine at Ora d'Aria, a Michelin-starred restaurant close to the banks of the Arno River, offering innovative Italian cuisine (€70 - €120).

Address: Via dei Georgofili, 11R, 50100 Firenze FI, Italy

  - ✓ Cap off the night with a private boat tour along the Arno under the stars (tour cost: €60).

DAY 4:

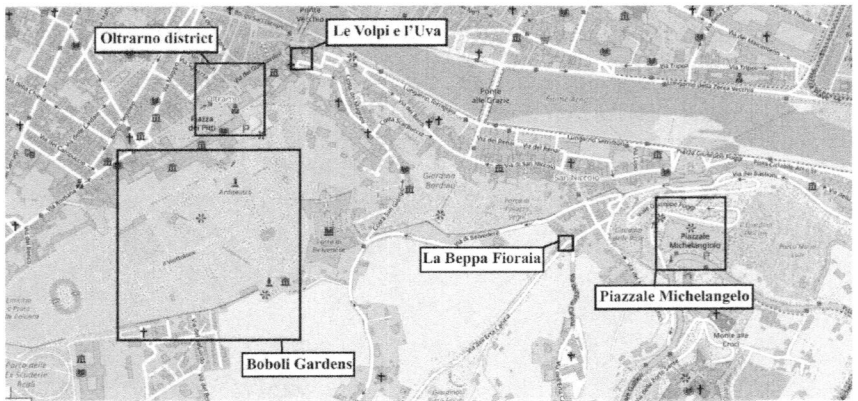

Day 4.

OpenStreetMap Contributors https://www.openstreetmap.org

✢ **Morning:**
- ✓ Visit the Boboli Gardens, but with a twist - experience a virtual reality tour to see the gardens through different historical periods (tour cost: €35).
- ✓ Lunch at La Beppa Fioraia, a charming restaurant with a garden terrace offering a mix of traditional and contemporary dishes.

Address: Via dell'Erta Canina, 6/R, 50125 Firenze FI, Italy

Boboli Gardens QR Code

- **Afternoon:**
  - ✓ Take a guided walking tour of the Oltrarno district, exploring hidden workshops and boutiques (tour cost: €25).
  - ✓ Indulge in a wine-tasting experience at Le Volpi e l'Uva, a cozy wine bar tucked away in a charming alley (tasting cost: €25).

Address: Piazza dei Rossi, 1R, 50125 Firenze FI, Italy

- **Evening:**
  - ✓ Conclude your extraordinary journey with a sunset visit to Piazzale Michelangelo, where you can reflect on the beauty of Florence beneath the changing hues of the sky.

Piazzale Michelangelo QR Code

CHAPTER 9
DAY TRIPS BEYOND THE CITY

Aside from the fact that Florence is the capital city of Italy's second-most-popular region for travelers, Tuscany, it is also globally known as a cradle to several Renaissance art and architecture masterpieces. The city is the most populated in the region, and it holds magic within its terracotta rooftops and cobbled streets. But, beyond the city's walls lie more sophisticated views. From the city of Florence, you can embark on unforgettable day trips that will give you a unique perspective on Italian life. These destinations are designed to cater to all kinds of interests, whether you're a lover of rich history, a foodie, a wine aficionado (someone who appreciates or collects wines), or you just admire breathtaking sceneries. All these are within easy reach for simple day trips.

Exploring beyond the walls of Florence is more than just crossing a checklist of attractions. It involves immersing yourself in the genuine pace of Tuscan life, unveiling secret treasures, and creating memories that'll last long even after you leave. This chapter will unlock the treasure chest of tourist attractions scattered just beyond the walls of Florence. Prepare to be captivated.

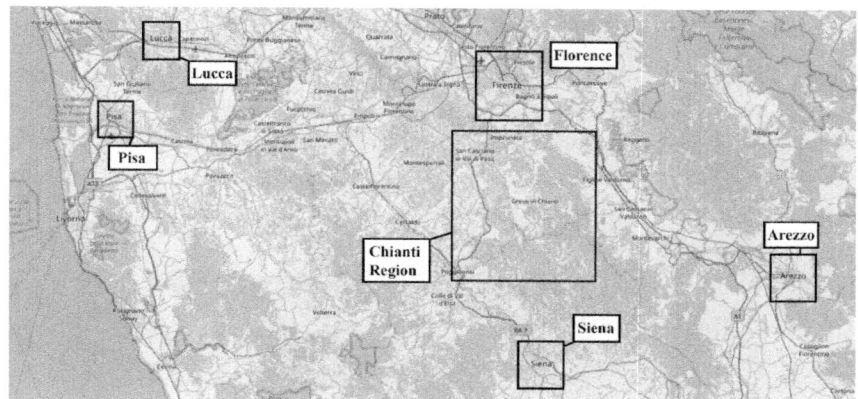

Day trips beyond the city.[56]

THE ENCHANTING TOWN OF SIENA

Siena became its own governed republic by the time it gained independence in the 12th century. The city is one of the oldest wonders in Tuscany, and it is primarily known for the several tourist attractions it holds, thanks to its artistic heritage. The city was founded by the sons of Remus, the brother of Romulus, who founded Rome, according to local legend.

Siena is one of the best places to visit in Tuscany. It is the magnificent medieval city to the south of Florence. This colorful town is well-known for its pici pasta and yearly horse race. Siena is the ideal destination for a short day adventure from Florence if you'd want to continue exploring Tuscany.

TRANSPORTATION OPTIONS

Most of the town's surroundings are tough to get to without a car, but Siena can easily be reached by train or bus.

Distance from Florence: 48.6 miles (78 kilometers)

TRAVEL TIME:

+ Approx. 1 hr by car.
+ Approx. 1 hr, 15 mins by bus.
+ Approx. 1 hr, 30 mins by train.

PLACES YOU SHOULD INCLUDE IN YOUR ITINERARY

Siena Cathedral: You can take a trip to one of the most beautiful churches in the world. It's the city's number-one tourist attraction and a must-visit in Tuscany. The mind-blowing cathedral houses the Piccolomini library, a small, remarkable space housing a wide collection of music books, with the walls painted in storytelling frescoes.

The Siena Cathedral is the city's number-one tourist attraction and a must-visit in Tuscany. [57]

Piazza Salimbeni: The Piazza Salimbeni is a small square surrounded by three magnificent palaces: Palazzo Salimbeni, Palazzo Tantucci, and Palazzo Spannocchi. The Palazzo Salimbeni used to be the home of the great Salimbeni family until their possessions were confiscated in 1419. To this day, the square houses the first bank in the world, the current Banca Monte dei Paschi di Siena.

The Central Piazza del Campo: This is the soul of Siena. It has a unique shell shape that is a masterpiece in the history of architecture. The Piazza del Campo is the largest medieval square in Italy and Europe. This is where some important events in the life of the Siena people take place, like the Palio Horse Racing, held on the 2nd of July and the 16th of August. It is also a spot where couples come to make their vows of love. It is also home to the *Fonte Gaia*, a beautiful fountain that further enriches the square.

Palazzo Pubblico: This is the castle-like structure that curves around the Piazza del Campo. The Palazzo Pubblico was uniquely designed to be the Republic of Siena's statehouse. A few decades after it was designed in 1297, the tall bell tower, Torre del Mangia, was attached to it. As of today, the Palazzo Pubblico, translated as "Public Palace of Siena," remains the city's town hall over eight hundred years later.

The Palazzo Pubblico was uniquely designed to be the Republic of Siena's statehouse. [58]

Museo Civico de Siena: If you're looking to explore Siena's finest treasures, then head over to the Civic Museum, located on the first floor of Palazzo Publico. On the walls and ceilings of the museum are priceless 13th-century frescoes, which are a must-see. You can also find paintings and sculptures done by 14th- and 15th-century artists from Siena here.

Some other must-see places in the enchanting town of Siena include:

+ *Piazza del Duomo*
+ *Loggia della Mercanzia*
+ *Chiesa di San Cristoforo*
+ *Torre del Mangia*

THE CHARMING TOWN OF LUCCA

The town of Lucca is rich in history, dating back to Ancient Roman times. The town is famous for its well-preserved Renaissance walls built in the 16th and 17th centuries and picturesque streets, perfect for cycling. The ancient walls of Lucca have been transformed into a pedestrian promenade that provides the perfect path for taking a stroll or a bike ride, offering breathtaking views of the town and its neighboring countryside.

The town of Lucca is also home to more than a hundred churches, including the renowned Lucca Cathedral (*Duomo di Lucca*) and the Basilica of San Frediano. One of the tourist attractions is the Guinigi Tower, where visitors usually flock to see the traditional Romanesque-Gothic architectural design and breathtaking views of the cityscape.

TRANSPORTATION OPTIONS

Lucca is a fairly small town in the region, so you either walk, rent a bike to cycle around, or take a taxi within its walls. However, public buses and trains are the most practical means of transportation for coming to the town or commuting to other parts of Tuscany. The train station in Lucca is situated on the southern outskirts, precisely two blocks beyond the fortifications at Piazza Ricasoli. The tourist office in the city of Lucca is situated adjacent to the bus station.

Distance from Florence: 50 miles (81 kilometers)

TRAVEL TIME:

+ *Approx. 1 hr by car.*
+ *Approx. 1 hr by bus.*
+ *Approx. 1 hr and 20 mins by train.*

PLACES YOU SHOULD INCLUDE IN YOUR ITINERARY

Lucca City Walls: Lucca's imposing and completely preserved city wall is one of the most important places to visit in the town. The wall has a length of about four kilometers, and it engulfs the entire city. There are about six ancient city gates that grant access to the city. The path created by the walls is stunning, and thanks to the many trees, a real recreation center was born. You can rent a bike and cycle around the historic center during your visit.

Lucca's imposing and completely preserved city wall is one of the most important places to visit in the town. [59]

Piazza dell' Anfiteatro: This should be your next stop when you're done admiring the walls. The Piazza dell' Anfiteatro is a large, circular piazza, once a Roman amphitheater dating back to the second century. It is a public square located in the northeast section of Lucca's walled historic center. The piazza is accessible through four gateways at each vertex of the ellipse. It is by far the most beautiful place in Lucca.

Torre Guinigi: Your visit to Lucca is not complete if you don't visit the Torre Guinigi Tower. It is one of the most important attractions in the town. The tower is 45 meters high and planted with trees. It has a significant impact on the cityscape of Lucca. Tourists make it a point to climb the tower during a city trip. This is an experience you don't want to miss out on. Once you get to the top of the tower, you'll be rewarded with the most spectacular viewpoint of the entire Lucca.

Palazzo Pfanner: If you're interested in beautiful gardens and palaces, then you should surely visit the Palazzo Pfanner. The magnificent building was built in the 16th century for the wealthy Moricani trading family. The palace is, however, named after its current owner, Felix Pfanner, who took over possession in the 19th century. The courtyard at Palazzo Pfanner is perfectly suited for holding events due to its magnificent scenic staircase and entrance hall boasting arched ceilings. Right in the middle of the garden is an enchanting fountain. The palace has now been converted into a museum of arts and artifacts, a must-see in the town of Lucca.

The magnificent building was built in the 16th century for the wealthy Moricani trading family. [60]

APPENDIX

This section includes an A to Z list of all attractions, monuments, museums, etc., mentioned throughout the book, with reference to the pages on which they are mentioned.

+ **Accademia Gallery, Centro Storico** – Mentioned in Chapters 6, 8
+ **Agriturismo Le Macine, Gavinana-Galluzzo** – Mentioned in Chapter 7
+ **Amerigo Vespucci Airport, Peretola** – Mentioned in Chapters 1, 2
+ **Antica Macelleria Falorni, Greve** – Mentioned in Chapter 9
+ **Antique Market, Arezzo** – Mentioned in Chapter 9
+ **Arezzo City, Tuscany** – Mentioned in Chapter 9
+ **Arezzo Park, Arezzo** – Mentioned in Chapter 9
+ **Arno River, Isolotto-Legnaia** – Mentioned in Chapters 1, 4, 6, 8 and 9
+ **Arnolfo Tower, Centro Storico** – Mentioned in Chapter 6
+ **Banca Monte dei Paschi di Siena, Siena** – Mentioned in Chapter 9
+ **Barberino Val d'Elsa** – Mentioned in Chapter 9
+ **Bargello Museo, Via del Proconsolo** – Mentioned in Chapter 8
+ **Basilica di San Miniato al Monte, Gavinana-Galluzzo** – Mentioned in Chapter 7
+ **Basilica of San Domenico, Arezzo** – Mentioned in Chapter 9
+ **Basilica of San Frediano, Lucca** – Mentioned in Chapter 9
+ **Bed and Breakfast Legnaia, Isolotto-Legnaia** – Mentioned in Chapter 4
+ **Boboli Gardens** – Mentioned in Chapter 8
+ **Boccanegra Restaurant, Campo di Marte** – Mentioned in Chapter 5
+ **Bologna City** – Mentioned in Chapters 1, 2
+ **Borgo Bottaia Hotel, Gavinana-Galluzzo** – Mentioned in Chapter 7
+ **Brolio Castle, Gaiole** – Mentioned in Chapter 9
+ **Cacio Vino Trallalla Bar, Campo di Marte** – Mentioned in Chapter 6

- **Campo di Marte District, East Florence** – *Mentioned in Chapters 2, 5*
- **Casa Buonarroti** – *Mentioned in Chapter 8*
- **Castellina Region** – *Mentioned in Chapter 9*
- **Castello Doria, Cinque Terre** – *Mentioned in Chapter 9*
- **Cemetery Campo Santo, Pisa** – *Mentioned in Chapter 9*
- **Centro Storico District, Central Florence** – *Mentioned in Chapters 6, 8*
- **Certosa di Firenze (Charterhouse), Gavinana-Galluzzo** – *Mentioned in Chapters 7*
- **Chianti Region, Tuscany** – *Mentioned in Chapters 2, 9*
- **Chiesa di San Cristoforo, Siena** – *Mentioned in Chapter 9*
- **Chiesa di San Frediano Church, Lucca** – *Mentioned in Chapter 9*
- **Cinque Terre Villages, Liguria region** – *Mentioned in Chapter 9*
- **Corniglia, Cinque Terre** – *Mentioned in Chapter 9*
- **Corso Italia, Arezzo** – *Mentioned in Chapter 9*
- **David by Michelangelo, Accademia Gallery, Centro Storico** – *Mentioned in Chapters 1, 6, 8*
- **Della Robbia Hotel, Campo di Marte** – *Mentioned in Chapter 5*
- **Duomo Cathedral, Centro Storico** – *Mentioned in Chapters 1, 2, 6, 8*
- **Duomo di Lucca, Lucca** – *Mentioned in Chapter 9*
- **Fiesole Town, Northern Florence** – *Mentioned in Chapter 1*
- **Florence Observatory, Campo di Marte** – *Mentioned in Chapter 5*
- **Florence Synagogue and Jewish Museum** – *Mentioned in Chapter 8*
- **Fonte Gaia Fountain, Siena** – *Mentioned in Chapter 9*
- **Fonterutoli Winery, Castellina** – *Mentioned in Chapter 9*
- **Fortezza Medicea, Arezzo** – *Mentioned in Chapter 9*
- **Gaio Clinio Mecenate National Archaeological Museum, Arezzo** – *Mentioned in Chapter 9*
- **Gaiole Region** – *Mentioned in Chapter 9*

- **Gavinana-Galluzzo District, South Florence** – *Mentioned in Chapters 7, 8*
- **Gelateria de' Coltelli, Pisa** – *Mentioned in Chapter 9*
- **Gelateria dei Neri, Centro Storico** – *Mentioned in Chapter 8*
- **Gelateria Legnaia, Isolotto-Legnaia** – *Mentioned in Chapter 4*
- **Giacomo Puccini's Birthplace, Lucca** – *Mentioned in Chapter 9*
- **Giardino dell'Orticoltura Garden, Campo di Marte** – *Mentioned in Chapters 3, 8*
- **Giotto's Bell Tower, Centro Storico** – *Mentioned in Chapter 8*
- **Grande Chiostro, Gavinana-Galluzzo** – *Mentioned in Chapter 7*
- **Gucci Garden** – *Mentioned in chapter 8*
- **Guinigi Tower, Lucca** – *Mentioned in Chapter 9*
- **Historic Center of Florence, Centro Storico** – *Mentioned in Chapters 1, 3, 6*
- **Hostel 7 Santi, Campo di Marte** – *Mentioned in Chapter 5*
- **I Porci Comodi, Pisa** – *Mentioned in Chapter 9*
- **Impruneta Village** – *Mentioned in Chapter 9*
- **Isolotto Market, Isolotto-Legnaia** – *Mentioned in Chapter 4 and Chapter 8*
- **Isolotto-Legnaia District, West-Southwest Florence** – *Mentioned in Chapters 4, 8*
- **La Beppa Fioraia Restaurant** – *Mentioned in Chapter 8*
- **La Giostra Restaurant** – *Mentioned in Chapter 8*
- **La Giostra Restaurant, Centro Storico** – *Mentioned in Chapter 6*
- **La Ménagère Restaurant** – *Mentioned in Chapter 8*
- **Le Volpi e l'Uva Bar** – *Mentioned in Chapter 8*
- **Leaning Tower, Pisa** – *Mentioned in Chapters 1, 9*
- **Legnaia Area, Isolotto-Legnaia** – *Mentioned in Chapter 4*
- **Leonardo da Vinci Museum** – *Mentioned in Chapter 8*
- **Loggia dei Lanzi Gallery, Centro Storico** – *Mentioned in Chapter 6*

- **Loggia della Mercanzia, Siena** - *Mentioned in Chapter 9*
- **Lucca City, Tuscany** - *Mentioned in Chapter 9*
- **Manarola, Cinque Terre** - *Mentioned in Chapter 9*
- **Mercato Centrale Market, Centro Storico** - *Mentioned in Chapter 6*
- **Mercato delle Pulci, Campo di Marte** - *Mentioned in Chapter 6*
- **Mercato di Gavinana, Gavinana-Galluzzo** - *Mentioned in Chapter 7*
- **Mercato di Rifredi Market, Rifredi** - *Mentioned in Chapter 3*
- **Monte Morello** - *Mentioned in Chapter 8*
- **Montefioralle Village** - *Mentioned in Chapter 9*
- **Monterosso, Cinque Terre** - *Mentioned in Chapter 9*
- **Museo Civico de Siena, Siena** - *Mentioned in Chapter 9*
- **Museo di San Marco** - *Mentioned in Chapter 8*
- **Museo di San Salvi, Gavinana-Galluzzo** - *Mentioned in Chapter 7*
- **Museo Galileo** - *Mentioned in Chapter 8*
- **Museo Stibbert, Isolotto-Legnaia** - *Mentioned in Chapter 8*
- **National Central Library, Santa Croce** - *Mentioned in Chapter 8*
- **Nelson Mandela Forum, Campo di Marte** - *Mentioned in Chapters 5, 8*
- **Officina Profumo-Farmaceutica di Santa Maria Novella Pharmacy, Centro Storico** - *Mentioned in Chapter 8*
- **Ospedale Meyer, Rifredi** - *Mentioned in Chapter 3*
- **Osteria del Ghiotto Restaurant, Rifredi** - *Mentioned in Chapters 3, 8*
- **Osteria della Bistecca Restaurant, Panzano** - *Mentioned in Chapter 9*
- **Osteria Santo Spirito Restaurant, Centro Storico** - *Mentioned in Chapters 6, 8*
- **Palace of Fraternita Dei Laici, Arezzo** - *Mentioned in Chapter 9*
- **Palazzo Blu, Pisa** - *Mentioned in Chapter 9*
- **Palazzo della Carovana, Pisa** - *Mentioned in Chapter 9*
- **Palazzo Mansi, Lucca** - *Mentioned in Chapter 9*
- **Palazzo Pfanner, Lucca** - *Mentioned in Chapter 9*

+ **Palazzo Pubblico, Siena** – *Mentioned in Chapter 9*
+ **Palazzo Salimbeni, Siena** – *Mentioned in Chapter 9*
+ **Palazzo Spannocchi, Siena** – *Mentioned in Chapter 9*
+ **Palazzo Tantucci, Siena** – *Mentioned in Chapter 9*
+ **Palazzo Vecchio Town Hall, Centro Storico** – *Mentioned in Chapters 1, 6, 8*
+ **Panzano Region** – *Mentioned in Chapter 9*
+ **Parco delle Cascine Park, Isolotto-Legnaia** – *Mentioned in Chapter 4*
+ **Parco Regionale delle Colline di Monte Morello, Gavinana-Galluzzo** – *Mentioned in Chapter 8*
+ **Pasticceria Vogel Pastry Shop, Isolotto-Legnaia** – *Mentioned in Chapter 4*
+ **Peretola Area** – *Mentioned in Chapter 2*
+ **Piazza Dalmazia Area, Rifredi** – *Mentioned in Chapters 3*
+ **Piazza dei Cavalieri, Pisa** – *Mentioned in Chapter 9*
+ **Piazza del Campo, Siena** – *Mentioned in Chapter 9*
+ **Piazza del Duomo, Pisa** – *Mentioned in Chapter 9*
+ **Piazza del Duomo, Siena** – *Mentioned in Chapter 9*
+ **Piazza dell' Anfiteatro, Lucca** – *Mentioned in Chapter 9*
+ **Piazza della Libertà, Arezzo** – *Mentioned in Chapter 9*
+ **Piazza di Galluzzo Area, Gavinana-Galluzzo** – *Mentioned in Chapter 7*
+ **Piazza Grande, Arezzo** – *Mentioned in Chapter 9*
+ **Piazza Napolene, Lucca** – *Mentioned in Chapter 9*
+ **Piazza Ricasoli, Lucca** – *Mentioned in Chapter 9*
+ **Piazza Santa Croce, Centro Storico** – *Mentioned in Chapters 1*
+ **Piazzale Michelangelo, Centro Storico** – *Mentioned in Chapters 6, 7, 8*
+ **Piccolomini Library, Siena** – *Mentioned in Chapter 9*
+ **Pisa Cathedral, Pisa** – *Mentioned in Chapter 9*
+ **Pisa City, Tuscany** – *Mentioned in Chapter 9*

- **Pitti Palace, Centro Storico** – *Mentioned in Chapters 6, 8*
- **Ponte della Maddalena, Lucca** – *Mentioned in Chapter 9*
- **Ponte Santa Trinita** – *Mentioned in Chapter 8*
- **Ponte Vecchio Bridge, Centro Storico** – *Mentioned in Chapters 1, 6, 8*
- **Portofino, Cinque Terre** – *Mentioned in Chapter 9*
- **Prato City** – *Mentioned in Chapter 2*
- **Residenza Gambrinus, Gavinana-Galluzzo** – *Mentioned in Chapter 7*
- **Rifredi District, North-Northwest Florence** – *Mentioned in Chapters 3, 8*
- **Rifredi Railway Station, Rifredi** – *Mentioned in Chapter 3*
- **Rifredi Theater, Rifredi** – *Mentioned in Chapters 3, 8*
- **Roman Amphitheater, Arezzo** – *Mentioned in Chapter 9*
- **Ruth's Kosher Vegetarian Restaurant** – *Mentioned in Chapter 8*
- **San Giovanni Battista Church, Isolotto-Legnaia** – *Mentioned in Chapter 4*
- **San Lorenzo Market** – *Mentioned in Chapter 8*
- **San Salvi Neighborhood** – *Mentioned in Chapter 8*
- **Santa Maria del Fiore Church, Campo di Marte** – *Mentioned in Chapters 1, 5*
- **Santa Maria della Pieve, Arezzo** – *Mentioned in Chapter 9*
- **Santa Maria Novella Train Station** – *Mentioned in Chapters 1, 2*
- **Santo Stefano dei Cavalieri Church, Pisa** – *Mentioned in Chapter 9*
- **Settignano Village, Northeast Florence** – *Mentioned in Chapter 1*
- **Siena Cathedral, Siena** – *Mentioned in Chapter 9*
- **Siena City, Tuscany** – *Mentioned in Chapter 9*
- **Sistine Chapel, Vatican City** – *Mentioned in Chapter 1*
- **Square of Miracles, Pisa** – *Mentioned in Chapter 9*
- **St. Peter's Basilica, Rome** – *Mentioned in Chapter 1*

- **Stadio Artemio Franchi Stadium, Campo di Marte** - *Mentioned in Chapters 1, 5, 8*
- **Teatro Cantiere Florida, Gavinana-Galluzzo** - *Mentioned in Chapter 7*
- **Teatro Comunale Theater, Centro Storico** - *Mentioned in Chapter 6*
- **Teatro del Sale Theater, Campo di Marte** - *Mentioned in Chapter 5*
- **Teatro della Pergola** - *Mentioned in the Chapter 8*
- **Teatro Obihall, Campo di Marte** - *Mentioned in Chapter 8*
- **Teatro Puccini Theater, Isolotto-Legnaia** - *Mentioned in Chapter 6*
- **Teatro Verdi, San Lorenzo** - *Mentioned in Chapter 8*
- **The Arezzo Cathedral, Arezzo** - *Mentioned in Chapter 9*
- **The Mudas Museum, Arezzo** - *Mentioned in Chapter 9*
- **Torre del Mangia, Siena** - *Mentioned in Chapter 9*
- **Torre delle Ore, Lucca** - *Mentioned in Chapter 9*
- **Trattoria Mario, San Lorenzo** - *Mentioned in Chapter 8*
- **Uffizi Gallery, Centro Storico** - *Mentioned in Chapters 1, 6, 8*
- **Vasari Corridor, Centro Storico** - *Mentioned in Chapter 6*
- **Vasari's House, Arezzo** - *Mentioned in Chapter 9*
- **Vernazza Harbor, Cinque Terre** - *Mentioned in Chapter 9*
- **Via dell'Amore, Cinque Terre** - *Mentioned in Chapter 9*
- **Via Reginaldo Giuliani Antique Shops, Rifredi** - *Mentioned in Chapter 3*
- **Via Ricasoli, Centro Storico** - *Mentioned in Chapters 1, 6*
- **Via Senese Street, Gavinana-Galluzzo** - *Mentioned in Chapter 7*
- **Viale dei Mille Area, Campo di Marte** - *Mentioned in Chapter 5*
- **Villa Fabbricotti Park, Rifredi** - *Mentioned in Chapter 3*
- **Villa Favard, Isolotto-Legnaia** - *Mentioned in Chapter 8*
- **Villa Le Piazzole, Gavinana-Galluzzo** - *Mentioned in Chapters 7*
- **Villa Medicea di Castello, Rifredi** - *Mentioned in Chapter 3*
- **Villa Strozzi Concept Store, Isolotto-Legnaia** - *Mentioned in Chapter 4*

- **Villa Strozzi Residence, Isolotto-Legnaia** – *Mentioned in Chapter 4*
- **Villa Strozzi, Isolotto-Legnaia** – *Mentioned in Chapter 4*
- **Villa Vogel, Isolotto-Legnaia** – *Mentioned in Chapter 4*
- **Volterra Town, Southwest Florence** – *Mentioned in Chapter 2*
- **Yellow Bar, Campo di Marte** – *Mentioned in Chapter 6*

CONCLUSION

> **Florence has not remained the city of yore. It has become more advanced and tourist-friendly, and at the same time, it has managed to retain its historical charm. The Florentines may be a proud people, but they also know how to give a heartfelt welcome to tourists from other parts of the world. Visiting Florence is not only an uplifting cultural and artistic experience but also a chance to explore authentic Italian hospitality.**

The first chapter started things off with a general overview of Florence, its location, history, evolution, culture and cuisine, famous celebrities, etc. Reaching the city is easy since it has its very own airport, but the alternative routes that lead to Florence are more than worth exploring, especially because of their scenic beauty.

Then, every district of the city was explored in vivid detail, starting with Rifredi, to the north. Florence may be catering to tourists in general, but Rifredi reveals the day-to-day lives of the locals. It has quite a few tourist destinations, too, like the Piazza Dalmazia and the Villa Fabbricotti.

Isolotto-Legnaia lies in the west-southwest part of Florence, which provides a singular blend of the modern and the ancient, as well as the urban and the natural. A captivating view of the Arno River can be found there, along with a few other sights, like the Parco delle Cascine and the Teatro Puccini.

Campo di Marte awaits to the east, where the city life truly starts to shine. It is an amazing mixture of science, sports, architecture, and modern life. The Florence observatory, the Stadio Artemio Franchi stadium, the Giardino dell'Orticoltura garden, and the Viale dei Mille market provide a little of everything to satiate the thirst of avid tourists.

Then comes the reason why everyone scrambles to visit Florence: the Centro Storico, in the heart of the city. It has some of the most iconic historical sites in the world, from the Duomo (cathedral) to the Palazzo Vecchio (town hall). It is the most crowded district of Florence during the tourist season, but the teeming crowd surprisingly enhances the beauty of its ancient architecture.

The final district in the south, the Gavinana-Galluzzo, is the quieter part of the city, in stark contrast to the center. It contains the Certosa di Firenze (charterhouse) and the Piazza di Galluzzo, along with other sights. A detailed itinerary and programs follow, along with the optimal timings. For those who wish to explore the sights beyond Florence, there is a thoroughly informative chapter near the end, as the book says its goodbyes with some useful Italian phrases and a long list of appendices.

If you enjoyed this book, a review on Amazon would be greatly appreciated because it would mean a lot to hear from you.

TO LEAVE A REVIEW:

1. Open your camera app.
2. Point your mobile device at the QR code.
3. The review page will appear in your web browser.

Or,

Click here to leave a review on Amazon

Thanks for your support!

Here's another book by Captivating Travels that you might like

Welcome Aboard, Discover
Your Limited-Time Free Bonus!

Hello, traveler! Welcome to the Captivating Travels family, and thanks for grabbing a copy of this book! Since you've chosen to join us on this journey, we'd like to offer you something special.

Check out the link below for a FREE Ultimate Travel Checklist eBook & Printable PDF to make your travel planning stress-free and enjoyable.

But that's not all - you'll also gain access to our exclusive email list with even more free e-books and insider travel tips. Well, what are you waiting for? Click the link below to join and embark on your next adventure with ease.

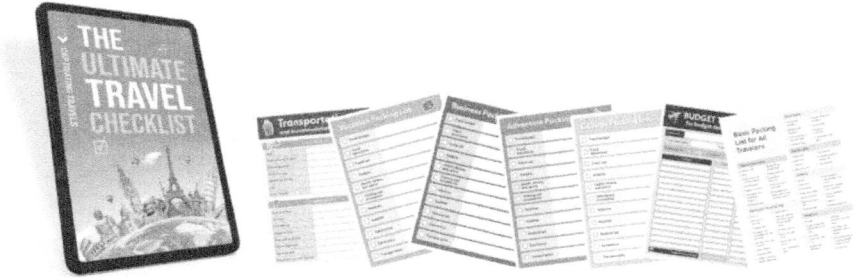

Access your bonus here: https://livetolearn.lpages.co/checklist/

Or, Scan the QR code!

REFERENCES

4 Days in Florence: A Perfect Itinerary for First-Time Visitors. (2023, December 1). Travel + Tannins - Travel and Wine Blog. https://travelandtannins.com/4-days-in-florence/

5 Best Restaurants in Rifredi, Florence. (n.d.). Quandoo. https://www.quandoo.it/en/firenze-rifredi

7 Best Restaurants in Gavinana / Galluzzo, Florence. (n.d.). Quandoo. https://www.quandoo.it/en/firenze-gavinana-galluzzo

ACD Communication & Creation. (2023). The Guide to Cinque Terre | mycinqueterre.com. MyCinqueTerre. https://www.mycinqueterre.com/

Benny, A. (2022, May 23). 5 Famous People from Florence Italy - As We Travel | Travel the World.https://aswetravel.com/famous-people-florence-italy/

Campo di Marte Travel Guide. (n.d.). TRIP.COM. https://www.trip.com/travel-guide/destination/campo-di-marte-2031977/

Chianti. (n.d.). Chianti, Land of Wine and Food. Www.visittuscany.com. https://www.visittuscany.com/en/areas/chianti/

Ciaoflorence Tours & Travel. (n.d.). Www.ciaoflorence.it. https://www.ciaoflorence.it/en/search-results?location=florence

Claudia. (13 Feb. 2023). How to Get from Bologna to Florence: 4 Best Ways. Myadventuresacrosstheworld.com. https://myadventuresacrosstheworld.com/how-to-get-from-bologna-to-florence/

ComPart Multimedia. (2023, June 26). Piazza Salimbeni - Siena, Italy. ItalyGuides.it. https://www.italyguides.it/en/tuscany/siena/piazza-salimbeni

Criscione, Candice. (22 Sept. 2023). Florence (Italy) Airport - Quick Guide for 2023-2024. The Tuscan Mom. https://www.thetuscanmom.com/florence-italy-airport/.

Culturetrip. (16 Feb. 2017) Foods You Must Try in Florence Italy. Culture Trip https://theculturetrip.com/europe/italy/articles/15-foods-you-must-try-in-florence-italy-

District 4 - Isolotto e Legnaia | Feel Florence. (n.d.). Www.feelflorence.it. https://www.feelflorence.it/en/node/16262

Djinis, Elizabeth. (9 June 2023). What It Means to Be Florentine. Italy Segreta. https://www.italysegreta.com/what-it-means-to-be-florentine/

Expedia.com. https://www.expedia.com/Rifredi.dx6141935

Farishta, N. (2023, May 4). 4 Days in Florence: Perfect Itinerary & Local Tips (2024). Globe Gazers - Solo Female Travel Blog | Life after Divorce. https://www.globe-gazers.com/4-days-in-florence/

Florence Peretola Airport (FLR) (11 Jan. 2024). Currency Exchange, Banks & ATMs. AirportBanking. https://www.airportbanking.com/florence-peretola-airport-flr/.

Florence Peretola Wheelchair Accessible Airport Transfers Disabled Facilities. Accessible Italian Holiday. https://www.accessibleitalianholiday.com/florence-peretola-airport-accessible-disabled-traveling-tuscany/

Flores, Lourdes. Getting to Florence by Air & Getting from the Airport to Downtown Florence. Www.visitflorence.com, www.visitflorence.com/getting-to-florence/by-air.html.

Folk Traditions in Florence | Feel Florence. https:// www.feelflorence.it, www.feelflorence.it/en/node/38591.

Gavinana - Galluzzo Travel Guide 2024 - Things to Do, What to Eat & Tips. (n.d.). TRIP.COM. https://www.trip.com/travel-guide/destination/gavinana-galluzzo-2035598/

GirlInFlorence. (2019, April 18). Eat, Drink, & Be Merry: Tips From a Local. Girl in Florence. https://girlinflorence.com/2019/04/18/restaurantsnightlife-list/

Greenaway, K. (n.d.). Things to Do in Campo di Marte: Florence Travel Guide by 10Best. 10Best. https://10best.usatoday.com/destinations/italy/florence/campo-di-marte/

Hansen, M. (2022, January 4). How to Spend 3 Days in Florence, Italy: A Complete Guide. Wheatless Wanderlust; Matt. https://wheatlesswanderlust.com/3-day-florence-itinerary/

Hill, E. (2022, April 29). How to Plan the Ultimate Florence to Siena Day Trip. Devour Tours. https://devourtours.com/blog/florence-siena-day-trip/?cnt=NG

Isolotto - Legnaia Travel Guide 2024 - Things to Do, What to Eat & Tips. (n.d.). TRIP.COM. https://www.trip.com/travel-guide/destination/isolotto-legnaia-2040065

Italia.it. (n.d.). Visit Florence: Things to Do & Attractions. Italia.it. https://www.italia.it/en/tuscany/florence

Johnston, A. (2021, July 23). A Florence Itinerary: 7 Days of Italian Bliss. Plum Guide. https://www.plumguide.com/journal/florence-itinerary-seven-days

Julie. (2023, February 17). 16 Amazing Things to Do in Arezzo (+ Map & Photos). Earth Trekkers. https://www.earthtrekkers.com/best-things-to-do-in-arezzo/

Julie. (2023, February 26). 2 Days in Florence Itinerary: Best Itinerary for First-Time Visitors. Earth Trekkers. https://www.earthtrekkers.com/2-days-in-florence-itinerary/

Juma. (2024, January 4). Top 15 Amazing Things to Do in Lucca (Italy). PlacesofJuma. https://www.placesofjuma.com/lucca-italy/

Katy. (16 June 2020). 101 Italian Phrases to Learn for Your Trip to Italy." Untold Italy. https://www.untolditaly.com/basic-italian-phrases-for-travel/.

Lensi, R. (2017, September 5). Florence - Centro Storico (Historic Center). Lensi Designs Photography; Robin Lensi. https://lensidesigns.com/florence-centro-storico-historic-center/

List of Sportspeople from Florence - FamousFix List. FamousFix.com. https://www.famousfix.com/list/sportspeople-from-florence.

Lourdes, Stefano, & Cristina. (2019). Tuscany, Italy 2019: Tourist Travel Guide to Holidays in Tuscany, Toscana - Discover Tuscany. Discovertuscany.com. https://www.discovertuscany.com/

Lourdes, Stefano, & Cristina. (n.d.). Itineraries in Florence: Ideas of What to Do and See in Florence, Italy. Www.visitflorence.com. https://www.visitflorence.com/itineraries-in-florence/

Lucy Dodsworth. (2021, October 20). On the Luce Travel Blog – Stylish, Affordable, and Sustainable Travel Experiences. On the Luce Travel Blog. http://ontheluce.com

Morgan-Grenville, G. (n.d.). The Best Places to Visit in Chianti. Www.redsavannah.com. https://www.redsavannah.com/journal/chianti-villa-holidays

Moving Around Florence by Taxi: Taxi Cabs in Florence. Www.visitflorence.com, https://www.visitflorence.com/moving-around-florence/by-taxi.html.

Nuss, R. (2023, October 5). 1 Day Florence Itinerary. Ruth Nuss; Rome by the Hour. https://ruthnuss.com/the-perfect-1-day-florence-itinerary/

Peveto, Tyson. (8 Sept. 2019). Top 10 Traditional Dishes of Florence. Cookly Magazine. www.cookly.me/magazine/europe/italy/florence/top-10-food-dishes-to-eat-in-florence-italy/.

Rifredi Novoli Florence & District 5: Rifredi Novoli and Brozzi in Florence. (n.d.). Holidayhomestuscany.com. https://www.holidayhomestuscany.com/tuscany-holidays-florence-rifredi-novoli-brozzi.html

Rifredi Travel Guide 2024 - Things to Do, What to Eat & Tips. (n.d.). Trip.com. https://www.trip.com/travel-guide/destination/rifredi-2032054/

Rome to Florence Train Tickets from US$3.40 | Rail Europe - Cheap Price. (n.d.) Www.raileurope.com. https://www.raileurope.com/en/destinations/rome-florence-train.

Rome2rio. (2019). Rome2rio: Discover How to Get Anywhere. Rome2rio. https://www.rome2rio.com/

Samantha. (2022, March 20). Florence Itinerary: A Guide for 3 Days. There She Goes Again. https://theresheegoesagain.org/florence-itinerary/

Sights in Florence's Historic Center. (n.d.). Reidsitaly.com. http://www.reidsitaly.com/destinations/tuscany/florence/sights/sights-centro.html

Stenger, Marianne. (11 July 2022). How to Learn Italian Fast: 23 Quality Tips Endorsed by Science. Berlitz. www.berlitz.com/blog/how-to-learn-italian-fast.

Steves, R. (2013, October 2). Florence Itinerary: Planning Your Time. Rick Steves. https://www.ricksteves.com/europe/italy/florence-itinerary

Stops and Things to Do on Pisa to Florence Drive or Road Trip. (31 Mar. 2023). Wanderlog. https://www.wanderlog.com/drive/between/9767/9630/pisa-to-florence-drive.

Tetraktys. (n.d.). Arezzo, Italy - An Insider's Guide to the Town of Arezzo in Tuscany, Italy. Love from Tuscany. https://lovefromtuscany.com/where-to-go/cities-in-tuscany/arezzo/

The District of Gavinana and Galluzzo | Feel Florence. (n.d.). Www.feelflorence.it. https://www.feelflorence.it/en/node/16261

The District of Rifredi. (n.d.). Feelflorence.It. https://www.feelflorence.it/en/node/16258

Things to Do in Rifredi in January (updated 2024). (n.d.). Trip.com. https://www.trip.com/travel-guide/attraction/rifredi-2032054/tourist-attractions/?locale=en-XX&curr=USD

Top Landmarks in L'Isolotto (Florence). (n.d.). Tripadvisor. https://www.tripadvisor.com/Attractions-g187895-Activities-c47-zfn15620691-Florence_Tuscany.html

Train from Rome Fiumicino Airport to Florence | ItaliaRail. Www.italiarail.com, www.italiarail.com/pages/routes/rome-fiumicino-airport-to-florence.

Tripadvisor LLC. (2023). Cinque Terre 2023: Best Places to Visit. Tripadvisor. https://www.tripadvisor.com/Tourism-g187817-Cinque_Terre_Italian_Riviera_Liguria-Vacations.html

UNESCO World Heritage Centre. (n.d.). Historic Centre of Florence. UNESCO World Heritage Centre. https://whc.unesco.org/en/list/174/

Yordanova, M. (2019, February 6). One Day in Pisa (Best Day Trip Itinerary 2022). My Vacation Itineraries. https://myvacationitineraries.com/one-day-in-pisa-itinerary/

IMAGE SOURCES

1. NiloGlock, CC0, via Wikimedia Commons: https://commons.wikimedia.org/wiki/File:Florence%27s_districts.svg

2. OpenStreetMap Contributors https://www.openstreetmap.org

3. https://commons.wikimedia.org/wiki/File:Medici_family_(Bronzino_atelier).jpg

4. https://commons.wikimedia.org/wiki/File:Aeroporto_di_Firenze_targhetta.jpg

5. NiloGlock, CC0, via Wikimedia Commons: https://commons.wikimedia.org/wiki/File:Florence%27s_5th_district_(Rifredi).svg

6. Sailko, CC BY 3.0 <https://creativecommons.org/licenses/by/3.0>, via Wikimedia Commons: https://commons.wikimedia.org/wiki/File:Piazza_dalmazia,_01.JPG

7. MelaniaMannelli, CC BY-SA 3.0 <https://creativecommons.org/licenses/by-sa/3.0>, via Wikimedia Commons: https://commons.wikimedia.org/wiki/File:Ospedale_Pediatrico_Meyer.jpg

8. Sailko, CC BY-SA 3.0 <http://creativecommons.org/licenses/by-sa/3.0/>, via Wikimedia Commons: https://commons.wikimedia.org/wiki/File:Giardino_dell%27Orticultura_7.JPG

9. Sailko, CC BY-SA 3.0 <https://creativecommons.org/licenses/by-sa/3.0>, via Wikimedia Commons: https://commons.wikimedia.org/wiki/File:Villa_fabbricotti,_04.JPG

10. cyberuly, CC BY 3.0 <https://creativecommons.org/licenses/by/3.0>, via Wikimedia Commons: https://commons.wikimedia.org/wiki/File:Teatro_di_Rifredi_-_Outside_-_Entrance.jpg

11. Sailko, CC BY-SA 3.0 <http://creativecommons.org/licenses/by-sa/3.0/>, via Wikimedia Commons: https://commons.wikimedia.org/wiki/File:Polo_delle_Scienze_Sociali_di_Novoli_06.JPG

12. I, Sailko, CC BY-SA 3.0 <https://creativecommons.org/licenses/by-sa/3.0>, via Wikimedia Commons: https://commons.wikimedia.org/wiki/File:Museo_stibbert,_interno_01.JPG

13 NiloGlock, CC0, via Wikimedia Commons: https://commons.wikimedia.org/wiki/File:Florence%27s_4th_district_(Isolotto-Legnaia).svg

14 91alex, CC BY-SA 4.0 <https://creativecommons.org/licenses/by-sa/4.0>, via Wikimedia Commons: https://commons.wikimedia.org/wiki/File:Nuovo_mercato_di_Piazza_dell%27Isolotto,_Firenze.jpg

15 I, Cyberuly, CC BY-SA 3.0 <http://creativecommons.org/licenses/by-sa/3.0/>, via Wikimedia Commons: https://commons.wikimedia.org/wiki/File:Villa_Strozzi_-_South_Facade_03.jpg

16 I, Cyberuly, CC BY 3.0 <https://creativecommons.org/licenses/by/3.0>, via Wikimedia Commons: https://commons.wikimedia.org/wiki/File:Chiesa_di_Sant%27Angelo_a_Legnaia_(Florence)_-_Overview_01.jpg

17 NiloGlock, CC0, via Wikimedia Commons: https://commons.wikimedia.org/wiki/File:Florence%27s_2nd_district_(Field_of_Mars).svg

18 Sailko, CC BY-SA 3.0 <https://creativecommons.org/licenses/by-sa/3.0>, via Wikimedia Commons: https://commons.wikimedia.org/wiki/File:Firenze,_museo_del_calcio,_ext.,_01.JPG

19 Sailko, CC BY 3.0 <https://creativecommons.org/licenses/by/3.0>, via Wikimedia Commons: https://commons.wikimedia.org/wiki/File:Firenze,_stadio_artemio_franchi,_campo_da_gioco,_07.jpg

20 Capricornis crispus, CC BY-SA 4.0 <https://creativecommons.org/licenses/by-sa/4.0>, via Wikimedia Commons: https://commons.wikimedia.org/wiki/File:Viale_dei_Mille_-_Vigevano_(incrocio_con_Corso_Torino).jpg

21 NiloGlock, CC0, via Wikimedia Commons https://commons.wikimedia.org/wiki/File:Florence%27s_1st_district_(Old_Town).svg

22 C messier, CC BY-SA 4.0 <https://creativecommons.org/licenses/by-sa/4.0>, via Wikimedia Commons: https://commons.wikimedia.org/wiki/File:Milano_Duomo_2392.jpg

23 Michelle Maria, CC BY 3.0 <https://creativecommons.org/licenses/by/3.0>, via Wikimedia Commons: https://commons.wikimedia.org/wiki/File:Florence,_Italy_Uffizi_Museum_-_panoramio_(5).jpg

24 Diego Delso, CC BY-SA 4.0 <https://creativecommons.org/licenses/by-sa/4.0>, via Wikimedia Commons: https://commons.wikimedia.org/wiki/File:Ponte_Vecchio_sobre_el_r%C3%ADo_Arno,_Florencia,_Italia,_2022-09-19,_DD_02.jpg

25 Jebulon, CC0, via Wikimedia Commons: https://commons.wikimedia.org/wiki/File:Palazzo_vecchio_Florence.jpg

26 TxllxT TxllxT, CC BY-SA 4.0 <https://creativecommons.org/licenses/by-sa/4.0>, via Wikimedia Commons: https://commons.wikimedia.org/wiki/File:Firenze_-_Florence_-_Piazza_della_Signoria_-_View_NW.jpg

27 Gallerie dell'Accademia, CC BY-SA 4.0 <https://creativecommons.org/licenses/by-sa/4.0>, via Wikimedia Commons: https://commons.wikimedia.org/wiki/File:Accademia_(Venice).jpg

28 Michael Wittwer, CC BY-SA 4.0 <https://creativecommons.org/licenses/by-sa/4.0>, via Wikimedia Commons: https://commons.wikimedia.org/wiki/File:Blick_auf_und_vom_Piazzale_Michelangelo_(LM28908).jpg

29 Aniello Bizzoco, CC BY-SA 4.0 <https://creativecommons.org/licenses/by-sa/4.0>, via Wikimedia Commons: https://commons.wikimedia.org/wiki/File:Firenze_-_Basilica_di_San_Miniato_al_Monte_-_2023-09-12_00-22-51_001.JPG

30 I, Sailko, CC BY-SA 3.0 <http://creativecommons.org/licenses/by-sa/3.0/>, via Wikimedia Commons: https://commons.wikimedia.org/wiki/File:Teatro_puccini,_interno_02.JPG

31 Ray in Manila, CC BY 2.0 <https://creativecommons.org/licenses/by/2.0>, via Wikimedia Commons: https://commons.wikimedia.org/wiki/File:The_Vasari_Corridor_Bridge,_Via_della_Ninna,_Florence.jpg

32 Sailko, CC BY-SA 3.0 <http://creativecommons.org/licenses/by-sa/3.0/>, via Wikimedia Commons: https://commons.wikimedia.org/wiki/File:Parco_delle_cascine,_anfiteatro.JPG

33 Felix König, CC BY 3.0 <https://creativecommons.org/licenses/by/3.0>, via Wikimedia Commons: https://commons.wikimedia.org/wiki/File:Cattedrale_di_Santa_Maria_del_Fiore_Florenz_M%C3%A4rz_2014.jpg

34 NiloGlock, CC0, via Wikimedia Commons: https://commons.wikimedia.org/wiki/File:Florence%27s_3rd_district_(Gavinana-Galluzzo).svg

35 Mongolo1984, CC BY-SA 4.0 <https://creativecommons.org/licenses/by-sa/4.0>, via Wikimedia Commons: https://commons.wikimedia.org/wiki/File:Chiesa_di_San_Lorenzo,_interno_(Certosa_del_Galluzzo)_01.jpg

36 Antonio del Pollaiuolo, CC BY 3.0 <https://creativecommons.org/licenses/by/3.0>, via Wikimedia Commons: https://commons.wikimedia.org/wiki/File:Piero_del_pollaiolo,_san_michele_arcangelo_e_il_drago,_ante_1465,_01.JPG

37 I, Sailko, CC BY-SA 3.0 <http://creativecommons.org/licenses/by-sa/3.0/>, via Wikimedia Commons: https://commons.wikimedia.org/wiki/File:Osservatorio_di_arcetri,_planetario_01.JPG

38 https://www.pexels.com/photo/a-person-holding-a-map-5966342/

39 OpenStreetMap Contributors https://www.openstreetmap.org

40 OpenStreetMap Contributors https://www.openstreetmap.org

41 OpenStreetMap Contributors https://www.openstreetmap.org

42 OpenStreetMap Contributors https://www.openstreetmap.org

43 OpenStreetMap Contributors https://www.openstreetmap.org

44 OpenStreetMap Contributors https://www.openstreetmap.org

45 OpenStreetMap Contributors https://www.openstreetmap.org

46 OpenStreetMap Contributors https://www.openstreetmap.org

47 OpenStreetMap Contributors https://www.openstreetmap.org

48 OpenStreetMap Contributors https://www.openstreetmap.org

49 OpenStreetMap Contributors https://www.openstreetmap.org

50 OpenStreetMap Contributors https://www.openstreetmap.org

51 OpenStreetMap Contributors https://www.openstreetmap.org

52 OpenStreetMap Contributors https://www.openstreetmap.org

53 OpenStreetMap Contributors https://www.openstreetmap.org

54 OpenStreetMap Contributors https://www.openstreetmap.org

55 OpenStreetMap Contributors https://www.openstreetmap.org

56 OpenStreetMap Contributors https://www.openstreetmap.org

57 © Raimond Spekking: https://commons.wikimedia.org/wiki/File:Duomo_di_Siena-9635.jpg

58 Ilaria Giuliodori, CC BY-SA 4.0 <https://creativecommons.org/licenses/by-sa/4.0>, via Wikimedia Commons: https://commons.wikimedia.org/wiki/File:Palazzo_Pubblico_dall%27alto.jpg

59 Giulia Trevisanello, CC BY-SA 4.0 <https://creativecommons.org/licenses/by-sa/4.0>, via Wikimedia Commons: https://commons.wikimedia.org/wiki/File:Mura_di_Lucca,_Particolare.jpg

60 Sailko, CC BY 3.0 <https://creativecommons.org/licenses/by/3.0>, via Wikimedia Commons: https://commons.wikimedia.org/wiki/File:Palazzo_pfanner,_giardini_03.jpg

61 https://commons.wikimedia.org/wiki/File:Montefioralle-Panorama1.jpg

62 John Samuel, CC BY-SA 4.0 <https://creativecommons.org/licenses/by-sa/4.0>, via Wikimedia Commons: https://commons.wikimedia.org/wiki/File:Exterior_of_the_Leaning_Tower_(Pisa)_02.jpg

63 https://unsplash.com/photos/white-neon-light-signage-on-wall-mZNRsYE9Qi4

Printed in Dunstable, United Kingdom